Coquihalla Country

Doug —
Congratulations on your
graduation — you've earned the
time to explore! Have fun.

An Outdoor Recreation Guide

Love from
Suan, Pat
and family.

by

Murphy Shewchuk

SONOTEK® PUBLISHING LTD.
P.O. Box 1752
Merritt, B.C. Canada V0K 2B0

First printing: December, 1990.
Revised and reprinted: July, 1991.

Canadian Cataloguing in Publication Data

Shewchuk, Murphy.
    Coquihalla Country

    Includes bibliographical references and index.
    ISBN 0-929069-02-1

    1. Outdoor recreation—British Columbia—Coquihalla
Region—Guide-books. 2. Coquihalla Region (B.C.)
—History—Guide-books. 3. Coquihalla Region (B.C.)
—Description and travel—Guide-books. 4. Natural
history—British Columbia—Coquihalla Region
—Guide-books. I. Title.
GV191.46.B75S5 1990   796.5'09711'72   C90-091716-4

SONOTEK® PUBLISHING LTD.
P.O. Box 1752,
Merritt, B.C.
Canada V0K 2B0

Telephone (604) 378-5930

Book design by Murphy Shewchuk.
Photographs and maps by Murphy Shewchuk unless otherwise credited. All illustrations are protected by copyright and may not be reproduced in any form without prior written consent of the publisher.
Printed in Canada by Peerless Printers, Kamloops, B.C.

Dedication

To Bridget and Katharine.

Acknowledgements

Coquihalla Country started off as an update to *Exploring the Nicola Valley*, originally published in 1981 by Douglas & McIntyre. However, as I began to retrace the routes that I had travelled a decade ago and several times since, I discovered a great many changes and a wealth of new information about the past and present. *Exploring the Nicola Valley* was to become merely a foundation for a book that would go beyond anything I had ever done before. What began as a simple summer project quickly grew into a major effort requiring thousands of kilometres of travel and hundreds of hours at the computer keyboard and in the darkroom.

Thanks to the encouragement of several *BC Outdoors* editors, including former editors Mary Aikins and Henry Frew, and present editor George Will, some of the building blocks were in place in the form of previously-published *Backroads* articles.

Much new material surfaced, however, delaying the project as each answer prompted new questions. Nancy Wise, Sonotek's distributor, encouraged me to continue even though deadlines had come and gone. Cecil Simpson and Stan Parkinson of BC Parks help with numerous "last minute" requests for information. Lorne Robertson of the Merritt Forest Service office also helped considerably with maps and information. Fellow hikers, including Jean Nelson, Jack and Wilma Grant, my wife Katharine and my grand-daughter Bridget, made the research trips much more worthwhile and interesting.

I would especially like to thank Katharine for her patience and understanding.

Murphy Shewchuk

●●●

3

Coquihalla Country

An Outdoor Recreation Guide

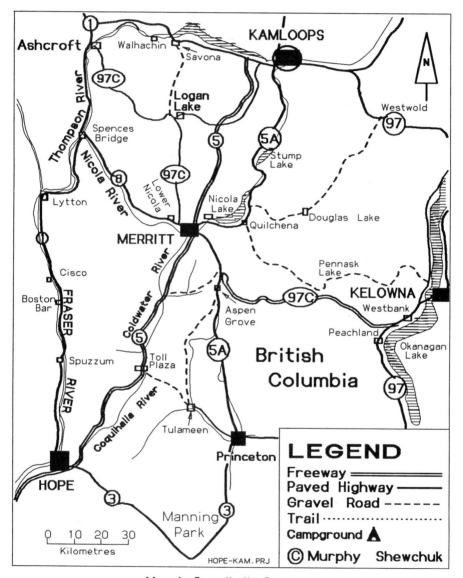

Map A: Coquihalla Country.

Table of Contents

Table of Contents

Maps

Photographs

Introduction

The heart of the Thompson Plateau and North Cascade Mountain region that has recently become known as *Coquihalla Country*, lies about three hour's drive to the northeast of Vancouver. It is bounded on the west and north by the Trans-Canada Highway and the Fraser and Thompson rivers, on the south by Crowsnest Highway 3 and the Similkameen River, and on the east by Highway 97 and the Okanagan Valley.

Coquihalla Highway 5 bisects the region from south to north and a second major highway, the Okanagan Connector (97C), ties the mid-point of the Coquihalla Highway to the Okanagan Valley. Highway 5A passes through the valley from Kamloops to Princeton, following the shorelines of many of the beautiful fishing lakes that lie along the lowland route. Highway 8 follows the Nicola River downstream from Merritt, through cultivated hay fields, market gardens and a narrow semi-desert canyon before reaching Spences Bridge on the Trans-Canada Highway.

Highway 97C, a recent designation to an old route, continues north from the Indian community of Shulus, on Highway 8 west of Merritt. Formerly the Mamit Lake Road, this route passes near the copper town of Logan Lake before winding northwest through the copper-rich Highland Valley and descending to Ashcroft on the Thompson River. To the north of the Logan Lake junction, a gravel road meanders through the lodgepole pine, past Tunkwa and Leighton lakes, before twisting down a steep hill into the village of Savona. To the east of Logan Lake, a paved route through the aspen and pine passes near Lac Le Jeune and descends to Kamloops on the Trans-Canada Highway. Countless dirt roads and trails branch off these more important routes.

A Canadian Pacific Railway spur line, formerly part of the famous Kettle Valley Railway, once provided a freight route from Penticton to the main line at Spences Bridge via Princeton and Merritt. The service was discontinued in May, 1989, with every indication that the rails will be removed.

Hope, at the southern gateway to *Coquihalla Country*, is a mere 154 km from Vancouver—1.5 hours from western Canada's largest population centre. Merritt, a city of 6,000 and the largest centre within the region, is only 270 km from Vancouver and 98 km from Kamloops, the northern gateway to the Coquihalla. Hope, Merritt and Kamloops have hotels, motels, campgrounds and most of the amenities appreciated by visitors.

The Thompson Plateau, which comprises the northern and eastern portions of *Coquihalla Country*, is a lake-dotted highland. The rounded, pine-covered mountains, open grasslands and many elongated lakes are clearly the result of ancient glacial action.

In contrast, the north slope of the Cascade Mountain chain that makes up the southwestern quarter of the region presents a startling change in topography and vegetation. Spire-like peaks reach for the sky. Cedar, spruce and hemlock fill the mountain valleys.

Anglers and hunters have long been aware of *Coquihalla Country's* many recreational attractions, but only in the past few decades have hikers, backpackers and cross-country skiers begun to explore the numerous trails. There is still much to be done before the vast potential of this rich and varied land is realized.

As an added note of caution, the dry grasslands of the Nicola Valley are a fragile environment and should be treated with respect. Please drive only on recognized roadways; the spring runoff or a sudden rainstorm can turn a hillside tire rut into a major gully, destroying the delicate rangeland.

Do not leave refuse behind. Stow it in the cans provided or take it out with you. A discarded bottle could start a fire in the hot summer sun or a discarded can could create a trap for wildlife.

Take nothing but photographs and memories and leave nothing but tracks—and be careful where you leave the tracks.

●●●

Important Notice!

Although every effort has been made to provide accurate information, road and trail conditions in *Coquihalla Country* are constantly changing. Consequently, neither the author nor the publisher can guarantee the continuing accuracy of details herein.

We do, however, look forward to your corrections to errors you may find and your comments on ways that you think this book may be improved. Please write the author in care of the publisher at the address listed in the front of the book.

●●●

Hope to Merritt

(Coquihalla Hwy 5)

Statistics	For map, see page 4.
Distance:	120 km, Hope to Merritt.
Travel Time:	One to two hours.
Condition:	Paved four to six lanes. Toll Highway.
Season:	Be prepared for snow near the Coquihalla Summit from October to May.
Topo Maps:	Tulameen 92 H/NE (1:100,000).
	Merritt 92I/SE (1:100,000).
	Yale 92H/NW (1:100,000).
	Chilliwack Lake 92H/SW (1:100,000).
Forest Maps:	Merritt - Princeton.
Communities:	Merritt & Hope.

The Coquihalla and Coldwater valleys have no significant settlements, yet they have been in almost continuous use as a transportation corridor since the mid-nineteenth century. In 1848-49, 20 km of the Coldwater valley near Merritt was part of a short-lived Hudson's Bay Company Brigade Trail from Kamloops to the Fraser River near Spuzzum. From 1849 to the early 1860s, the Coquihalla valley from Hope to Peers Creek received steady use as part of the Hope-Tulameen section of the Hudson's Bay Company Brigade Trail.

The Coquihalla valley saw little traffic after the completion of the Cariboo Wagon Road through the Fraser Canyon in the early 1860s. Traffic again picked up when a cattle trail was completed through the Coquihalla in 1876 at the request of Nicola Valley ranchers. The completion of the Canadian Pacific Railway in 1885 again left the Coquihalla in disuse except for a short burst of activity when the flood of 1898 wiped out the C.P.R. railway tracks in the Fraser Canyon.

The search for a route for a Coast-to-Kootenay railway led to completion of the Kettle Valley Railway through the Coquihalla Canyon in 1916. Heavy snowfall plagued the railroaders and despite some sixteen snowsheds, slides constantly threatened the crews, sometimes trapping them for a week or more. A mudslide wiped out a major bridge in 1959, permanently closing the line. Pipeline construction, begun before the rail line closed, then turned the valleys into primarily an oil and natural gas transportation corridor.

Lobbying by local residents for a new highway from Hope to Merritt began in earnest with the first Coquihalla Caravan on 21 July 1963. After facing the indignities of the extremely rough road over the old railbed, the conquering heroes were greeted at Hope by speeches, a pipe band and all the hoopla befitting a royal entourage. For the next decade, the Coquihalla Caravan was a major summer event, attracting participants from Kamloops and the Okanagan.

The lobbying continued until 13 January 1977 when, much to everyone's surprise, the provincial legislature announced "the design and construction of a highway from Merritt to Hope through the Coquihalla Pass." Two years later, in January 1979, Emil Anderson Construction of Hope was awarded a $4.3 million contract for the first five kilometres of the Coquihalla Freeway. Construction progressed slowly until the provincial government decided that this route to the B.C. Interior would be part of the showcase that was to become known as Expo 86. Crews began a 24 hour a day effort to meet the Expo deadline. Surveyors and designers barely kept ahead of earth-moving equipment and everyone lost sight of the original budget, but the new highway opened in May, 1986, in time to serve the Expo 86 tourist traffic.

Unfortunately the term "freeway" does not really apply to the Hope to Merritt section of the Coquihalla Highway. In an effort to make the vast expenditure more politically acceptable the route became British Columbia's first toll highway in modern history. Although tolls were once in effect on the Lions Gate and Second Narrows bridges in Vancouver, toll highways were discontinued when the Cariboo Wagon Road was finally paid off more than a century ago.

Highway exit numbers, introduced in the late 1980s, will serve as references to the various recreational attractions along the route.

Where justified, the major points of interest will be dealt with as separate chapters in this book.

Exit 170 (based on the number of kilometres from the Horseshoe Bay ferry Terminal in West Vancouver) is the junction between Highway 3 (The Crowsnest Route) and Highway 1 (The Trans-Canada Highway). It is the first major entrance to Hope and the point at which last-minute checks of fuel and supplies should be made for, except for roving tow-trucks prepared to pick up the unfortunate, there are no services available between Hope and Merritt.

Exit 177 marks the junction with Highway 3 and the beginning of Coquihalla Highway 5. To the west lies Manning Park, Princeton and the Okanagan Valley. To the north is the Coquihalla Highway through the Cascade Mountains, Merritt, Kamloops and points north and east.

Once over the hump that separates Nicolum Creek from the Coquihalla River, Highway 5 follows much the same route of the fur brigades, cattle drovers and Kettle Valley Railway. For the first few kilometres, that is, for Exit 183 (Kawkawa Lake Road) marks a parting of the ways. The old Hudson's Bay Company Brigade Trail continued east up Peers Creek and over Manson Ridge into the Sowaqua Creek drainage. (See *Manson Ridge Trail* for details.)

Five kilometres to the west of the intersection at Exit 183 the Othello (Quintette) Tunnels, built to traverse one of the narrowest constrictions in the Coquihalla Canyon, have been preserved as a provincial park. Barrie Sanford, in his book *McCulloch's Wonder*, details the almost miraculous efforts needed by Andrew McCulloch and the construction crews of the Kettle Valley Railway.

"Accepting this problem as merely another personal challenge, McCulloch daringly lowered himself and several of his fellow engineers in a small woven basket, suspended by ropes, down from the cliff tops into the canyon. There they cut narrow footholds in the rock walls upon which they could set up their survey instruments. After several weeks of such perilous work McCulloch confirmed his earlier suspicions. Instead of a single tunnel nearly a mile in length, McCulloch found that a line requiring barely a quarter as much tunneling could be cut directly through the canyon. McCulloch, moreover, chose an alignment which permitted the railway to cut not one, but five tunnels, thus exposing a multiple of working faces which greatly reduced the drilling time. Two bridges were to be built between three of the tunnels, each of them flush with the adjacent tunnel portals as a result of the abrupt drop to the river abyss below. More amazingly, all five tunnels and the two bridges were set on perfect tangent alignment. By accomplishing this alignment,

Fig. 1: Othello (Quintette) Tunnels near Hope.

McCulloch was able to push the tunnels - later known as the Quintette Tunnels - through the entire canyon with a scant third of a mile of trackage, literally *'threading the canyon... (of this) awe-inspiring gorge'*.

"On July 16, 1915 the Quintette bridges were finished and the tracklayers passed through the last of the five tunnels..."

Steel bridges and tracks were removed in the early 1960s after the railway discontinued operation through the Coquihalla. Bridging was restored by the Hope and District Chamber of Commerce in 1985-86, with the help of military engineers from Canadian Forces Base Chilliwack. The site was turned over to B.C. Parks in 1986. Since then, a parking lot, information shelter and toilets have been constructed within easy walking distance of the first tunnel.

Shylock Road (Exit 200) marks the point where the old railway right-of-way and the new Coquihalla Highway part company. The highway at this point is laid exactly where the tracks once carried steam-powered locomotives on their Coast-to-Kootenay run. The locomotives, however, continued to chug up the Coquihalla Canyon, clinging to the mountainside where no highway engineer dared build an all-weather high speed route. The highway instead takes a steeper course up the broader U-shaped Boston Bar Creek valley. Although the eight per cent grade would have been impossible for railway engines, it is only a slight inconvenience for today's traveller. The major advantages to this route are more room to build a multi-lane highway and fewer major snowslide zones.

Falls Lake (Exit 221) is a destination that is attracting hikers and fishermen, particularly since the hiking trail from the end of the road to the lake was completed in 1990. (See *Falls Lake Trail* for details.)

The Dry Gulch Bridge, one kilometre north of the Falls Lake exit, is the tallest of the 32 river, road or rail crossings in the 120 km-long-highway. A 175 metre steel arch spans the 90 metre deep gash in the mountain side.

The toll plaza, three kilometres farther north, marks the gateway to the Nicola Valley. The nearby Coquihalla Lakes drain south into the Coquihalla River, but the Coldwater River, which starts in the mountains to the west, drains north, joining the Nicola River at Merritt.

The Coquihalla Lakes exit (Exit 228) marks the departure point for several side trips and some excellent hiking or backpacking opportunities, each of which is dealt with separately. To the west is a forest access road into the heart of the Cascades (See *Upper*

Coldwater Road.) The road ends near the base of some challenging rock faces, but there is also an excellent hiking trail near the seven kilometre point into Little Douglas Lake that even the junior hiker can enjoy. (See *Little Douglas Lake Trail.*) To the east of the interchange forest roads lead into the headwaters of the Tulameen River and a variety of Forest Service recreation sites as well as a hiking trail along a portion of the old H.B. Co. Brigade Trail. (See *Tulameen River Road* and *Mount Davis Brigade Trail* for details.) Also to the east, the forest roads provide a shortcut to Tulameen with more Forest Service recreation sites for diversion. (See *Coquihalla-Tulameen Road.*)

Exit 228 also marks the return to the old railway right-of way. A steel bridge across the Coldwater River near the interchange was once used by the railway trains.

The Juliet Creek exit (un-numbered) 10 km north of the Coquihalla Lakes exit, is another point of departure from the humdrum travels of the paved highway. A short side road leads into a picnic site at the Coldwater River Provincial Park where stream fishing is a possibilty, but the serious backroads explorer and fisherman is more likely to tackle the forest road into Murray Lake, five kilometres to the northwest. Access from the Juliet Creek exit is steep and rough, so this backroad has been detailed from an easier access from Kingsvale on the Coldwater Road (Exit 256). (See *Murray Lake Road* for details.)

At the southern foot of Larson Hill (Exit 250) is the remnants of an old railway bridge that marks Brodie, the junction of the Kettle Valley Railway trackage to Hope, Princeton and Merritt.

The Coldwater Road also provides access to Brookmere, a tiny community once a maintenance point on the K.V.R. and another backroad to the alpine ridges of Thynne Mountain, both of which are covered later. Cross-country skiing trails and fine fishing lakes in the Kane Valley are also accessible from the Kane Valley Road near Kingsvale as well as from Highway 5A /97C, south of Merritt.

Comstock Road (Exit 276) provides access to another fishing lake and the top of Iron Mountain. (See *Gwen Lake Road.*) Then its another 10 km to floor of the Nicola Valley and Merritt. With the completion of the Okanagan Connector (97C) route in 1990, Exit 286 became a major junction in the Coquihalla system. This exit also provides access to Merritt and points west via Highway 8. A second interchange, Exit 290, provides access to Nicola Lake and the old Kamloops-Merritt route via Highway 5A.

For a detailed look at attractions along the various routes, see the appropriate sections.

●●●

16

Manson Ridge Brigade Trail

(Peers Creek Road)

Statistics   For map, see page 19.

Distance:	6.5 km Coquihalla Hwy to end of road (900826).
Travel Time:	One half hour.
Condition:	Rough road, dry weather only.
Season:	Summer and early fall.
Topo Maps:	Chilliwack Lake 92 H/SW (1:100,000).
	Hope 92 H/6 (1:50,000).
Forest Maps:	Chilliwack - Hope.
Communities:	Merritt & Hope.

Exit 183 (Kawkawa Lake) on Coquihalla Highway 5 about 10 km north of Hope provides access to one of the last remaining sections of the historic Hudson's Bay Company Brigade Trail through the Cascade Mountains. This trail from Fort Hope to Kamloops was the main route of commerce to the B.C. Interior from 1849 until 1860 when the Fraser River gold rush prompted the construction of a wagon road through the Fraser Canyon.

According to Bob Harris and Harley Hatfield in *Old Pack Trails in the Cascade Wilderness*, Alexander Caulfield Anderson made the first recorded trip through the Cascades in 1846. Anderson was in search of a new route from Kamloops to the Pacific Ocean that would replace their trail to the mouth of the Columbia River now impeded by the new U.S. boundary at the 49th parallel.

Anderson left the Fraser River at what is now Hope and followed much the same route as Crowsnest Highway 3 to Snass Creek, north of Rhododendron Flats. He followed Snass Creek upstream, continuing north up the east fork to the Cascade divide overlooking a pretty round lake that he named *The Punch Bowl*. This alpine pond was at the headwaters of the Tulameen River, and Anderson followed the Tulameen down through its narrow canyons to Otter Lake. Near the present village of Tulameen, Anderson met the Indian chief "Blackeyes" who told him that, but for the snow, he would have seen Blackeyes' much easier trail running directly over the Tulameen Plateau.

Based on his initial experience, Anderson later recommended a trail from Yale to the Nicola Valley via the Anderson River, Uztlius Creek, Midday Creek and the Coldwater River. The Kequeloose Trail, as it was known, proved unsatisfactory because of the dangerous Fraser River crossing and a lack of feed for the pack horses.

Henry Peers was assigned the task of finding a new route through the mountain barrier and he chose to explore the second major Coquihalla tributary northeast of Hope. Peers' route ran parallel to Anderson's, but to the north. Following the creek that now bears his name up to its source, he crossed Manson Ridge and descended into the Sowaqua basin via Fool's Pass and a sloped, wooded ridge that angled to the valley floor near the mouth of Matthew Creek. Peers' trail then climbed Mount Davis and descended into the headwaters of the Podunk, a tributary of the Tulameen River. (See the **Mount Davis Brigade Trail** section for details.) After reaching the Tulameen, he followed Blackeyes' trail over the top of the Tulameen Plateau and down to Otter Lake. From "Campement des Femmes", near present-day Tulameen, the overland route to Kamloops was relatively easy.

Peers' trail was the main route of commerce to and from the interior from 1849 to 1860, when the discovery of gold in the upper reaches of the Fraser River prompted the construction of a wagon road through the nearly impassable Fraser Canyon. New railway and highway routes replaced the Hudson's Bay Co. Brigade Trail and it had almost disappeared when, in the late 1970s, **Opportunities For Youth** work crews began rebuilding it under the auspices of the Okanagan Similkameen Parks Society.

As late as 1981, the Brigade Trail from Lodestone Lake, at the top of the Tulameen plateau, to the head of Peers Creek—a distance approximately 80 km—was total wilderness. Since that time, logging roads have been built across it near the headwaters of the Podunk and in the upper reaches of the Sowaqua. What was once a week-long hike can now be broken up into manageable sections, although wilderness hiking experience is still an essential requirement.

18

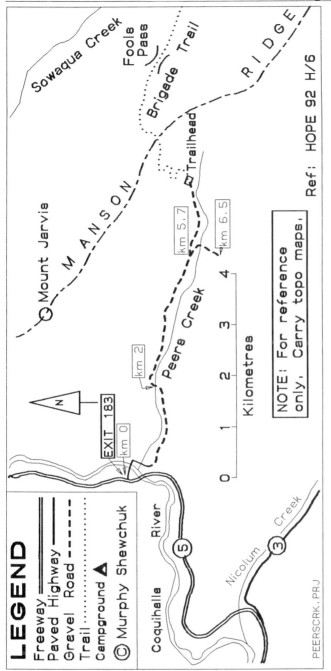

Map 1: Peers Creek / Manson Ridge HBC Trail.

To reach the start of the trail up Manson Ridge, take Exit 183 (Kawkawa Lake Road) and cross over to the east side of the Coquihalla River. With the interchange as your km 0 reference, follow the Peers Creek Forest Road upstream, crossing the bridge to the north side of the creek at km 2. The rough, narrow road climbs steeply for the next two-to-three kilometres, gaining almost 500 metres. Stay on the main road, keeping right at a junction at km 4.7, until a junction at km 5.7. Here the main road continues along for about 300 metres to major creek crossing (Peers Creek) and ends at a washout half a kilometre later. The side road to the left at km 5.7 leads up to the Manson Ridge trail head. In late August, 1990, it was passable with a 4x4 with lots of clearance although it had been ditched in a dozen places to direct the spring runoff across the road.

If your vehicle has limited clearance, park part way up the side road or at a wide area on the main road near the creek crossing. It is about a 45 minute hike to the trail head and another one to two hours to the top of the ridge. At the time of writing, there were no signs at the start of the trail. It begins, however, at the log landing at the end of the road and is marked with red squares tacked to the trees and a small white metal sign designating it as the Hudson's Bay Co. Brigade Trail.

The journal of Lt H.S. Palmer, RE describes his climb up 1450 metre high Manson Ridge from Manson Camp (the present trail head) in mid-September, 1859: "Rose at dawn, and soon commenced the laborious ascent of the Mountain by a zigzag trail... After struggling up this difficult mountain path for an hour and a half, we reached the summit of the pass, the magnificent view from which fully compensates... for the labour... As far as the eye could reach, an endless sea of mountains rolled away into blue distance... How we were ever to get out of them appeared to me somewhat difficult of solution..."

Lt. Palmer's views were not always as beautiful on that trip, for he also reports: "Mr. McLean of the Hudson Bay Company, who crossed in 1857 or 1858, on the 16th of October, had a very disastrous trip, and lost 60 or 70 horses in the snow... in riding over the mountain, and more particularly on its eastern slope, my horse frequently shied at the whitened bones of some one of the poor animals... left to perish where he lay."

The trail breasts the ridge near the west end of a long natural clearing. Various game trails follow the ridge to the east, providing access to alpine meadows and some excellent views of the lower Fraser Valley and the Cascade Mountains to the north. The trail down to Fool's Pass and Sowaqua Creek may be difficult to locate in places because of logging and new growth. Until more work is done on it, I do not recommend it except to the experienced mountain backpacker/explorer.

●●●

Falls Lake Trail

Statistics   For map, see page 22.

Distance:	1.1 km from Coquihalla Hwy to trail head. Approximately 1 km trail head to Falls Lake.
Travel Time:	Hiking time approximatetly 15 minutes.
Condition:	Good walking trail.
Season:	All season. Beware of snowslides in spring.
Topo Maps:	Spuzzum 92 H/11 (1:50,000).
Forest Maps:	Merritt - Princeton.
Communities:	Merritt & Hope.

Fig. 2: Falls Lake.

Falls Lake takes its name from beautiful Bridal Veil Falls that was a famous K.V.R. landmark in the Coquihalla Canyon. One of the last remaining wooden bridges in the old Kettle Valley line straddles Fallslake Creek below the cliff near Exit 221. Unfortunately, the bridge is not easily seen except from the rough gravel road that follows the old railway right-of-way through the canyon.

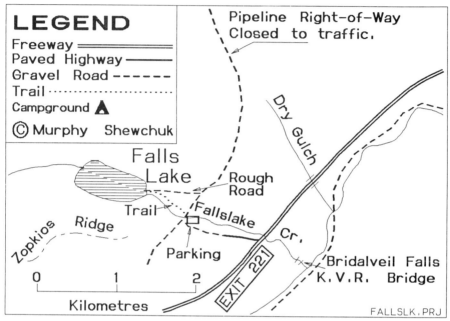

Map 2: Falls Lake Trail.

Falls Lake, however, is much more accessible, particularly since an excellent walking trail was completed into the lake in the summer of 1990. For the first few minutes, the trail climbs an old skid road, then it enters the heavy timber where the undergrowth resembles a coastal rainforest—without Devil's Club. Boardwalk bridges traverse the small creeks and log-reinforced steps make the undulating terrain easy to navigate.

The elevation gain is minor. The parking lot is at 1250 metres, only slightly higher than the 1244 metre summit of the highway. The lake is at 1300 metres and the trail climbs little more than 10 metres above lake level as it skirts the cliffs.

Trout fishing, the easy walk and the cool mountain air are the prime attractions of Falls Lake.

●●●

Coquihalla — Tulameen Road

For map, see page 26.

Statistics

Distance:	40 km Coquihalla Hwy 5 to Tulameen.
Travel Time:	One to two hours.
Condition:	Gravel with a few rough, narrow sections.
Season:	Dry weather during summer and fall.
Topo Maps:	Tulameen 92 H/NE (1:100,000).
	Princeton 92 H/SE (1:100,000).
Forest Maps:	Merritt - Princeton.
Communities:	Merritt, Hope & Tulameen.

There is a backroad shortcut from Coquihalla Highway 5, near the Toll Plaza, to the community of Tulameen that can save you a few hours of travelling as well as give you a chance to explore some new terrain—if conditions are right. Conditions in the Cascade Mountains are dependent on a number of factors, most important of which are season and weather. The best time to travel through this area is summer and early fall, but sudden storms on the higher ridges can change conditions quickly.

The only way to travel safely is to be prepared for the worst. Don't head into the mountains without an axe or saw. Do make sure your fuel tank is full before you start. If the weather turns foul, be prepared to turn around. Don't try to compete against Nature. Discretion, it has been said, is the better part of valour.

Coquihalla Lakes Exit 228 on Coquihalla Highway 5, a short distance north of the Toll Plaza, is the departure point for the Britton Creek Rest Area as well as several other interesting backroad trips. The road to the village of Tulameen begins as the Tulameen River Forest Service Road a few hundred metres south of the Rest Area entrance.

Fig. 3: East Murphy Lake.

With the junction near the old K.V.R. "Y" as the km 0 reference, follow the gravel road to east of Coquihalla Lake. The road leaves the Coquihalla Valley near km 2 and begins a steady climb up Britton Creek as it continues south and then east. A junction near the 8K signpost marks a name change for the route to Tulameen. The Tulameen River Forest Service Road to the right continues up into the headwaters of the Tulameen River. (See Tulameen River Road for details.) Follow the Lawless-Britton Creek Forest Road to the left as it continues a southeasterly course along Britton Creek.

A junction to the right at km 11.1 marks a road down to the west end of the Murphy Lakes and a Forest Service recreation site a short hike from the lakeshore. The road continues to climb as it swings away from Britton Creek, offering an excellent view of the Murphy Lakes at km 14.5 and a hidden junction to the Murphy Lake East rec site at km 16.2—just before the 8K marker.

The Murphy Lake East rec site has few redeeming features, but there is an interesting one-kilometre-long trail through the timber to the lake. Parts of the trail follow a long-abandoned road with quite easy grades that suggest that it may have even been part of a logging railway route.

The road now swings northwest, then north before crossing Skwum Creek at km 20.3. Keep right and across the bridge unless you are looking for a dead-end road to camp or try a little hunting. From Skwum Creek the road traverses the sidehill before descending to Lawless Creek at km 22.8. There are several openings near the creek for self-contained camping—carry a shovel, for biffies are in short supply. One of these openings is the access road to a placer mining operation that was active a few years ago.

After crossing Lawless Creek, the road begins a switch-back climb up the side of Mount Rabbitt. A junction at a turn at km 24.6 marks another change in identity as the road becomes the Lawless Creek Forest Service Road. Keep right and you will soon note that the roadside kilometre markers are beginning their countdown to Tulameen. The road crests at an elevation of about 1450 metres and begins the long brake-burning descent to Tulameen. Keep to the old road past a new forest road and some ranches and you should reach Tulameen via the Lawless Creek Road about 40 kilometres after leaving the Coquihalla Lakes area.

If you are planning to take this shortcut from the east end, follow 2nd Street in Tulameen west to Lawless Creek Road.

●●●

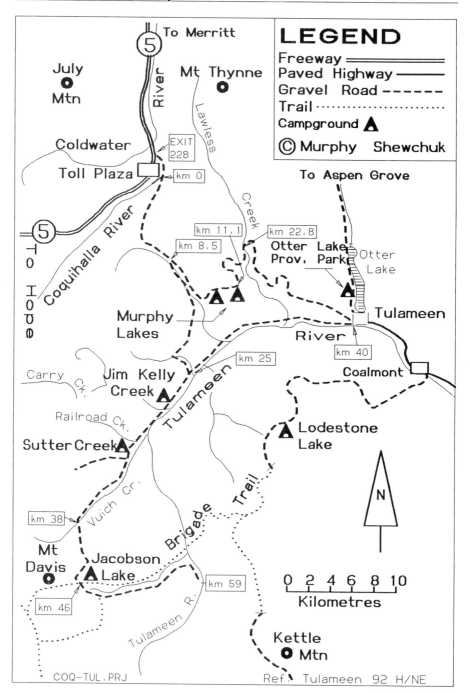

Map 3: Coquihalla / Upper Tulameen Area.

Tulameen River Road

Statistics	For map, see page 26.
Distance:	60 km from Coquihalla Hwy to end of road.
Travel Time:	One to two hours in dry weather.
Condition:	Gravel road with rough sections.
Season:	Summer and early fall.
Topo Maps:	Tulameen 92 H/NE (1:100,000).
	Princeton 92 H/SE (1:100,000).
Forest Maps:	Merritt - Princeton.
Communities:	Merritt & Hope.

I had mixed feelings when I learned that the Forest Service and Merritt's Tolko Industries Ltd. had extended the Tulameen River Road up Vuich Creek and across Podunk Creek at roughly the mid-point of the Tulameen-Hope section of the historic Hudson's Bay Company Brigade Trail. The wilderness aspect was now lost but access was improved. Obviously there would be winners and losers in the multiple-use concept of sharing natural resources. As a backroads explorer, I am a winner, for the road opens up some extremely scenic mountain country. As a wilderness hiker, I am a loser, for now the sounds of the chain saw and the trail motorcycle are an unwelcome part of the environment.

Forestry and the Coquihalla Highway have both improved access to the Cascade Mountains, but not without opposition. The Okanagan Similkameen Parks Society has waged a lengthy campaign to preserve the last remaining wilderness section of the old Hudson's Bay Company Brigade Trail. The H.B.Co. used the rugged trail from 1848 to 1860 as a trade route from Hope to Kamloops, hauling furs and trade goods on packhorses over the mountain passes.

Katharine and I hiked this route in 1980 and 1981 as part of a small group of sometimes-maligned supporters of the historic and wilderness trails in southwestern B.C. Both trips were challenging, rewarding, strenuous and certainly unforgettable. Easy is one description that wouldn't fit for the seven-day, 80-kilometre walk across the Cascade Mountains.

Armed with the new Forest Service Recreation Sites map for the Merritt-Princeton area and a couple of old topographic maps (92 H/NE and 92 H/SE), we set out, on a midsummer Friday afternoon, to find out what had happened to "our" wilderness. We left the Coquihalla Highway at the Coquihalla Lakes Interchange (Exit 228). Then we followed the signs to the Britton Creek Rest Area before continuing south for about 0.2 kilometres to the start of the Tulameen River Forest Road.

The junction here is at the site of an old Kettle Valley Railway spur where the engines were turned around or parked after pulling the freights up the steep Coquihalla Canyon from Hope. By using the higher Boston Bar Creek valley, the new Coquihalla Highway bypasses the toughest and most scenic section of the old railway route.

Tulameen River Road is a well-used logging road and caution is important, particularly on weekdays. For the purposes of this backroad adventure, the junction near the north end of Coquihalla Lake is km 0. The road soon swings to the east of Coquihalla Lake into huckleberry country. Logging and forest fires, some of them caused by the fire-belching steam locomotives of the Kettle Valley Railway, kept the forest from squeezing out the shrubbery. In my early research on the history of the valley, I discovered a newspaper report of hundreds of pounds of huckleberries being picked by the Natives near Coquihalla Pass.

Look closely at the brush along the roadway and you just might see the flicking ears of a mule deer or the brown face of a bear — you may also come face-to-face with a herd of cattle lounging in the middle of the roadway.

The first important junction is at km 8.5 where the road to the left winds its way past the Murphy Lakes and over the mountains to the village of Tulameen. (See the Coquihalla—Tulameen Road for details.) The Tulameen River Road swings to the right, crosses Britton Creek and winds its dusty way through several logged areas before offering the first glimpse of the upper Tulameen canyon near km 15.

Side roads in the area are confusing because the logging activity often makes them appear better than the main route. We passed up one of these near km 16, but took an unplanned diversion on another near km 19 — only to end up at a washout a kilometre later. The kilometre number signs on the roadside trees should be watched carefully. An unexpected change in sequence could mean you've left the main route.

A junction at km 25 marks the old road down the Tulameen Canyon to Tulameen village. Just to cause confusion, a sign at the junction clearly marked it to "Coalmont". To further compound the problem, a bridge a little more than halfway along the canyon road, is (was?) about to collapse because of rotting log beams. There were clear indications of surveys and foundation drilling for a replacement bridge and, according to highway maintenance sources, plans are underway to replace it.

We kept to the right at km 25, continuing up the Tulameen River past the Champion Creek Road junction at km 26 and Jim Kelly Creek recreation site near km 27. The canyon road climbs steadily, passing through several freshly logged areas.

Railroad Creek, at km 32, is one of these boulder-strewn waterways. The creek, according to Barrie Sanford in McCulloch's Wonder (p.p. 55-57), was part of one of three railway routes from Hope to Princeton put forward by Edgar Dewdney in 1901. This route would have followed the Tulameen River upstream from Princeton, through the village of Tulameen, and up through the canyon to Railroad Creek before crossing Railroad Pass and following Unknown (Carry) Creek down to the Coquihalla River. Although considerably shorter than the route adopted a decade later, the grades were just too steep for Railroad Pass to receive serious consideration.

Although the change is not obvious at first, the forest road leaves the Tulameen River halfway between Kelly Creek and Railroad Creek and begins following Vuich Creek into the heart of the Cascade Mountains. Ministry of Environment signs mark an important hunting boundary near km 38 with vehicular hunting prohibited beyond this point. The road crosses Vuich Creek and begins a steady climb through an old burn to Jacobson Lake at km 45.5.

The last 40 kilometres was new territory to us, but now memories began to return — memories of slogging along the old Brigade Trail and an evening walk along the shores of tiny Jacobson Lake in the summer of 1980. It took two and a half days of hiking to get here from the end of the road at Lodestone Lake and now we could drive in from the Coquihalla Highway in little more than an hour. We pulled our VW Vanagon into the recreation site at Jacobson Lake and settled in for the evening. When the full moon cast its eerie light through the cool mist a few hours later, memories of a darker night in a damp tent on a lumpy meadow flooded back.

The Tulameen River Road crosses the Brigade Trail at km 46, and after hearty breakfast we donned somewhat lighter packs than on the previous excursion and set out to find out if Palmer Pond was still on Mount Davis. (See Mount Davis Brigade Trail for details.) After a very short swim in the cool, clear waters of Palmer Pond, (elevation 1830 metres (6000 ft)) we retraced our steps to the Jacobson Lake recreation site for a pleasant afternoon of fishing and photography.

On our final day in the upper Tulameen, we continued to the end of the road at approximately km 59. After crossing Podunk Creek near the Brigade Trail junction, the road swings east and down Podunk Creek to the Tulameen River. Except for a well-hidden crossing of the old Rice Trail, the remainder of the road has few redeeming features.

Backroad explorers should find the Tulameen River Road interesting for several reasons. First and foremost, in my mind, is the relative ease of access to the heart of the Cascade Mountains. A close second is the number of camping options including small Forest Service Recreation Sites. Lake and stream fishing opportunities exist although not at a significant level. Back-country hikers may also wish to take advantage of the fact that the road bisects the old Brigade Trail and use the Jacobson Lake recreation site as a midpoint access to the Lodestone Lake to Peers Creek section of the wilderness trail.

●●●

Mount Davis Brigade Trail

Statistics	For map, see page 34.
Distance:	4.5 km, Jacobson Lake to Palmer Pond.
Hiking Time:	Two to three hours.
Elevation Gain:	300 to 350 metres.
Condition:	Some steep, muddy sections.
Season:	Best in late August.
Topo Maps:	Hope 92 H/6 (1:50,000).
Forest Maps:	Merritt - Princeton.
Communities:	Merritt & Hope.

The Mount Davis section of the Hudson's Bay Company Brigade Trails is undoubtedly the most scenic and pristine part of what remains of a major route of commerce. It is also of historical interest from at least two perspectives. Over this route, from 1849 until 1860, horse brigades brought the furs to the Pacific Coast from as far away as Stuart Lake, all bound for Qua-Qua-Alla, the present site of the town of Hope.

Accompanying the Kamloops Brigade in July, 1855 was Paul Fraser, Chief Trader from Fort Kamloops. Fraser was an autocratic tyrant with an uncontrollable temper. His cruel ruthlessness was probably influenced by his association with Chief Trader Donald Manson, a man noted for his ill-treatment of the men.

Earlier in 1855, Fraser had severely beaten one of the men at Fort Kamloops, a French Canadian named Farlardeau. The man died two days later and, on the day of his death, Fraser passed the carpenter shop where an Iroquois, Baptiste, was planing a board. Fraser asked the reason for the work.

"A coffin for Farlardeau," replied Baptiste.

"Well," said Fraser, "don't waste anymore time on that, rough boards are good enough for him."

The Iroquois was astounded at this remark and, after a stoic stare at his master, replied with candid frankness, "When you die you may not even get rough boards to be buried in!"

Two months later Chief Factor James Douglas received a letter from Donald Manson, dated July 7th, 1855, which contained in part "...I have at this moment (1 p.m.) arrived here from Qua-Qua-Alla, where I left Mr. McLean at 6 a.m. this morning with our Brigade. I am sorry to inform you of the death of an able and worthy friend - Chief Trader Paul Fraser. Poor gentleman, he only survived the blow about an hour. He never spoke. I shall see that he is interred as well as our means permit."

Chief Factor James Douglas's report to the Hudson's Bay Company's secretary dated July 25th, 1855 adds more detail. "Letter arrived from Langley announces the death of Chief Trader Paul Fraser at the Encampment de Chevruil. A tree fell on him and he survived only about an hour."

There is some doubt that the death, which took place at their camping place on the south slopes of what is now called Mount Davis, was purely accidental. Paul Fraser was in his tent resting after a hard day on the trail and the men were continuing to prepare the camp for the evening, when the tree being cut for firewood or bed boughs fell on the tent, narrowly missing Donald Manson who was also on that particular Brigade. From the standpoint of the men, neither man would have been mourned for long.

Podunk Davis, whose name is now attached to the mountain and a creek that drains the alpine meadows, was a major participant in a story that had a happier ending—at least where the Cascade Trails are involved.

According to D.M. Waterman in an article in the 1976 40th Report of the Okanagan Historical Society (Nurse Warburton pp 73-74) Mary Warburton was a nurse who worked in Vancouver in the winter months and picked fruit in the Okanagan Valley during the summer. Nurse Warburton had a penchant to hike the Hope-Princeton (Dewdney) Trail and was not easily deterred by the saner heads around her.

In 1926, this determined woman set out on foot from Hope. After ten days her sister in Vancouver became alarmed when she received no word of her arrival in Princeton. The police were alerted and search parties were formed at Hope and Princeton. Over two weeks passed with no sign of the missing nurse, and all hopes faded.

Suddenly the word spread that she had been found. When she explained her circumstances to D.M. Waterman, she told of being led astray by well-used game trails and of finding an old trapper's cabin just when she thought all was lost. After resting, she had set out again in search of the trail when "I suddenly saw a white-haired figure approaching me through the trees... my first thought was that it was the Angel Gabriel..."

Fig. 4: Hikers on the H.B.C. Brigade Trail.

The "Angel Gabriel" was none other than "Podunk" Davis, an impressive looking trapper and guide, who had continued the search for Miss Warburton on his own after all hope had been abandoned. For his persistence and ultimate success, Podunk Davis was awarded the Royal Canadian Humane Association Medal.

A year or more later, Nurse Warburton succeeded in conquering the Hope-Princeton Trail. However, it is a fitting finale to Miss Warburton's story that she vanished with scarcely a trace on the Squamish-Indian River Trail in October, 1931.

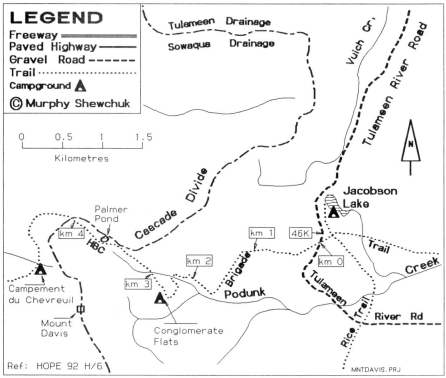

Map 4: Mount Davis HBC Brigade Trail.
Adapted from Forest Service and topographical maps.

The H.B.C. Brigade Trail from Jacobson Lake to Palmer Pond, at the crest of Mount Davis, and down to Campement du Chevreuil should pose few of the hazards that Mary Warburton faced—although game trails are plentiful.

The trail begins 100 metres past the 46K marker on the Tulameen River Road, less than a kilometre south of Jacobson Lake. (See the Tulameen River Road section for details.) There is little room for parking near the trail head, so vehicles are best left at the recreation site at Jacobson Lake. The starting elevation is about 1500 metres (according to my pocket altimeter) and the trail climbs steadily westward from the road as it skirts a semi-open rocky knoll. A fire, believed to have taken place in the 1930s, has stripped much of the old-growth timber from this slope, leaving new growth interspersed with a carpet of huckleberry bushes and other shrubs.

After about 1.5 km, the trail gradually descends to a small creek and a meadow before beginning the serious climb up to Conglomerate Flats. Before reaching the flats, the trail crosses the north fork of Podunk Creek (elevation. 1650 m) just below a rocky canyon. Then the trail swings south and up into a beautiful open meadow dotted with large conglomerate (puddingstone) boulders. Marmots, pikas and deer—and maybe a few elk—make this meadow home. It is also an excellent location for a lunch break or wildflower photography break. In mid-August, 1990, we identified rare butterwort (Pinguicula vulgaris), an insectivorous violet-like flower plus fields of monkeyflower, Indian paintbrush and red mountain heather.

The trail skirts the meadow to the northeast, before cutting through a narrow stand of timber and into a sloped snowslide path. At the three kilometre point it emerges at the foot of a long narrow meadow just above the rocky canyon that carries Podunk Creek. The trail may be a little difficult to trace as it winds up the right (north) side of the meadow through a waist-deep field of hellebore, but the destination is Palmer Pond, just over the horizon at the top of the meadow. Approach the crest of the meadow with care and you may see deer lunching on the slopes.

Palmer Pond, named after Lt H.S. Palmer, RE who kept a detailed diary of his trip through the area in September, 1859, is another good place for a break. The lake is beautifully clear and round and—at 1800 metres—understandably cool should you decide to take a swim. A game trail through the juniper thicket near the cutlet of the lake leads to an excellent view of Montigny Creek, almost 600 metres straight down. To the north lies the red slopes of 2156 metre Tulameen Mountain.

The trail angles across the slope above the lake and around the north side of the mountain, climbing another 50 metres before it begins a 200 metre descent along a hogs-back ridge to Chevreuil Creek and Campement du Chevreuil.

The trail through the alpine and along the edge of the cliffs above Palmer Pond is easy to lose. Watch for survey ribbons and red metal flags on the trees. Horses are occasionally used on the trail, so hoof prints and horse manure are sure signs that you have found the trail.

It is easy to understand why Campement du Chevreuil was one of the favoured overnight stops for the Brigades. The clear stream flows down off Mount Davis, even in mid-summer and there is plenty of shelter in the trees and plenty of grass in the meadows.

In mid-August, the open slopes to the north of the camp are an extended berry patch of giant proportions. I found time to enjoy the afternoon sun and nibble away on huckleberries, low bush blueberries and wild strawberries—all from one resting spot.

Fig. 5: A grouse searches for her chicks.

Beyond Campement du Chevreuil, the Brigade trail winds westward across the slope before making a switchback descent to Sowaqua Creek near the mouth of Matthew Creek. We explored the route to the edge of the mountain overlooking the Sowaqua in 1990, but have not hiked down to the valley floor since 1981. Road building equipment could be seen near Sowaqua Creek, so it is safe to say that you could reach the forest road there, should you not want to retrace your steps to Jacobson Lake.

●●●

Upper Coldwater Road

Statistics	For map, see page 42.
Distance:	Approximately 15 km to end of road.
Elevation Gain:	250 metres.
Travel Time:	One half hour.
Condition:	Gravel road, some rough sections.
Season:	Summer and early fall. Also suitable for skiing.
Topo Maps:	Spuzzum 92 H/11 (1:50,000).
Forest Maps:	Merritt - Princeton.
Communities:	Merritt & Hope.

Take a close look at a map of the area to the west of the Coquihalla Lakes and you may be surprised to see the unusual names that adorn the craggy peaks and ridges. According to Pat Lean in Place Names of the Nicola Valley (Nicola Valley Archives Association Newsletter/Historical Work Paper July 1978) the group of mountains that surround the headwaters of the Coldwater and Anderson rivers received their strange names in the late 1970s.

George M. Dawson's "Preliminary Report of the Physical and Geological Features of the Southern Portion of the Interior of British Columbia - 1877", published by the Geological Survey of Canada in 1879, (pp 37-38) describes the area in this manner:

"About the junction of the Uz-tli-hoos and Anderson, the mountains have an average elevation of between 5,000 and 6,000 feet. Looking up the Valley of the Anderson, a great block of higher mountains at a distance of about thirteen miles, can be seen. On the west of the group is an irregular conical peak, nearly vertical on one side. These summits must reach an altitude of 7,000 to 8,000 feet. West of the immediate vicinity of the Coldwater, on this line, no country suitable for stock-raising or farming exists. Fine timber

37

occurs in some of the valleys, as in all those of streams draining the eastward slopes of the Cascades. Here, however, it is almost inaccessible..."

Although Dawson does not appear to have assigned a name to these mountains, Amos Bowman may have done so in 1882-84. The name Anderson River Mountains assigned originally to the whole group seems officially to have been reduced to the one peak referred to by Dawson "an irregular conical peak, nearly vertical on one side..."

However, in December 7, 1975 nearly 100 years after Dawson's visit, Philip Kubic, a mountaineer from West Vancouver, put forth a proposal to have the individual mountain peaks officially named. The request was based on the confusion caused to mountaineers by the lack of official names and included a whole series of proposed names. Kubic's proposal was accepted by the Canadian Permanent Committee on Geographical Names.

In naming these mountains, Philip Kubic chose the names of ruminants, (animals that chew their food twice) who inhabit alpine regions of the world. These he divided into 3 groups. European for the most westerly mountains; American for the center group of features; and Asian for the easterly group. They follow in alphabetical order:

Alpaca Peak Between headwaters of Coldwater and Anderson Rivers. Alpacas are domesticated relatives of Vicunas and Guanacos.

Anderson River Mountain Lying to the north west of the group of mountains this is probably the one specific feature pointed out by Dawson in 1877. In writing about it in 1975 Kubic stated: "Unfortunately the name Anderson River Mountain doesn't fit into the scheme but I think that this isn't a serious drawback. All of the peaks that I have proposed names for are granitic. Anderson River Mountain, however, is composed of a type of brown rock quite different from granite. Geologically, Anderson River Mountain is unrelated to its neighbors. This peak, of course, takes its name from the Anderson River which was named in honor of Alexander Caulfield Anderson. (See *Manson Ridge Trail* for more information.) It is interesting to note that this mountain was indicated on Anderson's map compiled in 1867 with the words "Conical Peak."

Bighorn Peak Near the headwaters of the East Anderson River. The name refers to the Rocky Mountain Bighorn sheep.

Chamois Peak To the east of Anderson River and just to the south of Anderson River Mountain. A Chamois is a small horned species of antelope which inhabits the Alps. This name is particularly suited to be used in British Columbia since a chamois or "shammy," being the leather made from the skin of a Chamois, was used by the placer miners of this colony to separate the gold from quick-silver. This was part of the refining process in the early days.

Gamuza Peak To the east of Anderson River. The most southerly of the western group of peaks. Gamuza is the Spanish work for Chamois.

Gemse Peak Second range of peaks to the east of Anderson River. Gemse is German for Chamois.

Guanaco Peak At the headwaters of the Coldwater and East Branch of Anderson River. A Guanaco is a species of Llama inhabiting the Andes from Peru to Tierra del Fuego.

Ibex Peak To the east of the Anderson River. To the south of Chamois Peak. An Ibex is a species of goat with very long curved horns That inhabits the Alps.

Llama Peak At the headwaters of the Coldwater and Anderson Rivers. Llamas are domesticated relatives of Vicunas and Guanacos.

Nak Peak Above Zopkios Ridge, near the headwaters of the Coldwater River and to the west of the Coquihalla River. A Nak is a female Yak.

Reh Peak One of that group of eight peaks lying to the east of Anderson River and to the south and west of an unnamed branch of Anderson River. A Reh is a deer which inhabits the foothills of the Alps. The source of the word is German.

Serna Peak To the south and west of Reh Peak. Serna is Russian for Chamois.

Steinbok Peak To the south and east of Anderson River Mountain. Steinbok is the German term for Ibex.

Thar Peak The most easterly of three peaks rising above Zopkios Ridge. Lies wholly within the Falls Lake, Coquihalla River watershed. A Thar is Himalayan animal similar to a Chamois. It is a species of goat-like antelope inhabiting high inaccessible mountains in Europe and western Asia. It is about the size of a well grown goat and extremely agile.

Vicuna Peak At the headwaters of the Coldwater River and East Anderson River. A Vicuna is a species of Llama inhabiting the mountains of Peru, Bolivia and Colombia. The Vicuna is highly valued as a source of wool.

Yak Peak One of the three peaks rising above Zopkios Ridge at the head of the Coldwater River and to the west of the Coquihalla River. A Yak is a horned wild ox inhabiting Tibet and the Himalayas.

Zoa Peak Lies at the headwaters of the Coldwater and Fallslake Creek. A Zoa is the female offspring of a bovine bull and a Nak.

Fig. 6: Vicuna Peak, in the upper Coldwater.

Zopkios Ridge A ridge lying to the north of Nak, Yak and Thar Peaks at the headwaters of Boston Bar Creek and Fallslake Creek. A Zopkios is either the male or female offspring of a bovine bull and a Nak.

Zum Peak Lies completely within the several branches that form the headwaters of the Coldwater River. A Zum is the female offspring of a bovine bull and a Nak.

Zupjok Peak At the headwaters of Boston Bar Creek, Anderson River and Coldwater River. A Zupjok is the male offspring of a bovine bull and a Nak.

Philip Kubic is to be commended for his efforts towards having these features properly designated. His originality certainly has added color to the place names of British Columbia.

Exit 228, which provides access to the Tulameen area, also allows you to explore the upper reaches of the Coldwater River. Head west, across the Coquihalla Highway on the overpass if you are coming from the south, and cross the Coldwater River on a steel-sided bridge that once served the Kettle Valley Railway. With this bridge as your reference. you will reach the end of pavement at the Emcon Services highway maintenance yard near km 1 and begin the gravel Forest Road that winds into the heart of the mountains.

The road crosses the Coldwater River again near km 2.5. Just downstream from the bridge, the Coldwater makes a wide swing in high water, creating an island. In low water, if you are willing to risk getting stuck in loose gravel, you can drive down the stream bed and camp on the island. Carry a shovel and be extremely careful with fire as there are no facilities on this island.

Keep to the right at a junction near km 4.5 and follow the main valley upstream through several logged areas. A small Forest Service recreation site at a creek crossing just past the 7K sign marks the entrance to the hiking trail into Little Douglas Lake. See *Little Douglas Lake Trail* for details.)

Upper Coldwater Road then swings to the north around Zum Peak before continuing southeast up to the headwaters of the Coldwater River. A junction in the middle of the valley near the 13K sign marks a side road up to a cut block on the eastern slopes of Vicuna and Guanaco peaks. In the summer of 1990, the road ended at an elevation of approximately 1350 metres, in a cut block about 15 km from the Coquihalla Highway. Skidder trails led to the upper fringes of the timber, a short hike from the sheer granite slopes of Llama and Alpaca peaks.

Although you are never far from logging cuts, the huckleberries, new growth and easy access to some spectacular mountain peaks does make it a little easier to accept.

●●●

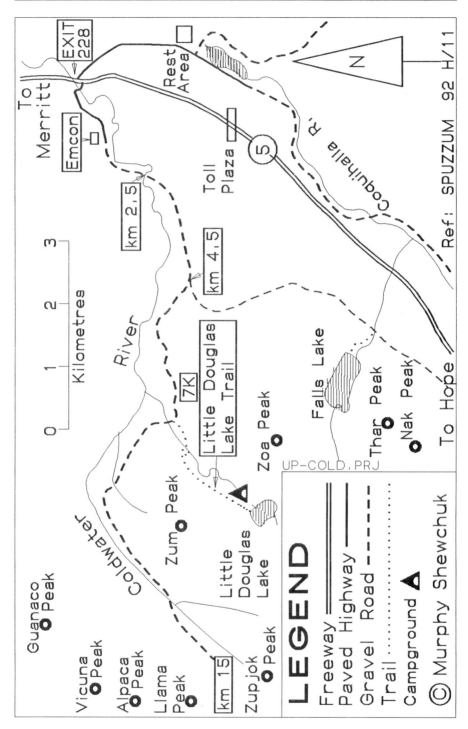

Map 5: Upper Coldwater / Little Douglas Lake Area.

Little Douglas Lake Trail

Statistics	For map, see page 42.
Distance:	Approximately 2 km, trail head to lake.
Elevation gain:	Approximately 100 metres.
Travel Time:	30 to 40 minutes.
Condition:	Well-marked forest trail.
Season:	Summer and early fall.
Topo Maps:	Spuzzum 92 H/11 (1:50,000).
Forest Maps:	Merritt - Princeton.
Communities:	Merritt & Hope.

Fig. 7: Little Douglas Lake, looking southwest.

Little Douglas Lake is surrounded on three sides by jagged mountain ridges reaching as high as 1830 metres—a jewel in a rough-hewn setting. Although less than an hour's walk from the Upper Coldwater Road, the tall timber and high ridges surrounding the lake easily hide the scars of civilization.

The Little Douglas Lake Trail and a rudimentary campsite near the outlet of the lake were first brushed out in 1977. At that time there were also plans to continue the trail up the north ridge and along the crest of Zopkios Ridge to the outlet of Falls Lake. The second part of the plan has so far not happened, but the Forest Service has continued to improve the trail and the campsite at the lake. Zum Peak Recreation Site at the trail head was moved about 20 metres and rebuilt during the summer of 1990.

The Little Douglas Lake Trail begins at Zum Peak Recreation Site, located at a bridge on the Upper Coldwater Road, approximately 7.5 km from Coquihalla Highway 5. The trail initially meanders through a shoulder-high jungle of fireweed and shrubs, including plenty of black huckleberry bushes. Note that consideration is being given to relocating the trail into the timber closer to the creek, where it was several years ago, and it may follow the creekside route by the time you read this.

After two or three hundred metres, the trail enters the timber and crosses the stream before climbing up to a bench on the northwest side of the valley. It is then an easy walk through the forest to the lake. Hemlock, cedar, ferns and the occasional devil's club line the two-kilometre-long trail, but it is not overgrown as some of the coastal trails can be. Total hiking time is 30 to 40 minutes, depending on conditions and distractions.

Little Douglas Lake is nearly circular with a small sheltered bay on the southeast corner. The glacial silt has built a marsh on the northeast side, but the rocky slopes on the north and south provide easier access to open water for a little trout fishing. Don't expect any lunkers as the trout seen from shore appear to be little more than 25 cm long.

•••

Brookmere Road

Statistics   **For map, see page 46.**

Distance:	10 km, Coquihalla Hwy 5 to Brookmere.
	25 km, Coquihalla Hwy 5 to Coalmont Road.
Travel Time:	15 min. to Brookmere. One hour to Coalmont Rd.
Condition:	Gravel with some rough sections.
Season:	Summer only, Brookmere to Coalmont Rd.
Topo Maps:	Aspen Grove 92 H/15 (1:50,000).
Forest Maps:	Merritt - Princeton.
Communities:	Merritt & Hope.

Louis H. Brooks and Phillip P. Brooks were the first settlers in the community now known as Brookmere, registering their lots in 1909. In the spring of 1911, it appeared that both the Kettle Valley Railway and the Vancouver, Victoria and Eastern Railway and Navigation Company would be running lines from Princeton to the coast via the pass where the Brooks had there farms.

Plans were immediately set in motion for the survey of a large new town on Louis Brooks' land. The agreement called for the railway company and Brooks to each get half of the 360 surveyed lots. Brooksville, it was said, would have a very advantageous position at the summit of Pass Creek (now Brook Creek) and Spearing Creek, the west fork of Otter Creek.

Brooksville became Brookmere, some say because of the swamp on which the town was built. It did become a divisional point for the Kettle Valley Railway, but the major community never did materialize. Today about a dozen homes are occupied and Brookmere has the distinction of having the last remaining K.V.R.

water tank still standing—although it had to be moved off its original foundation to save it from the wrecker.

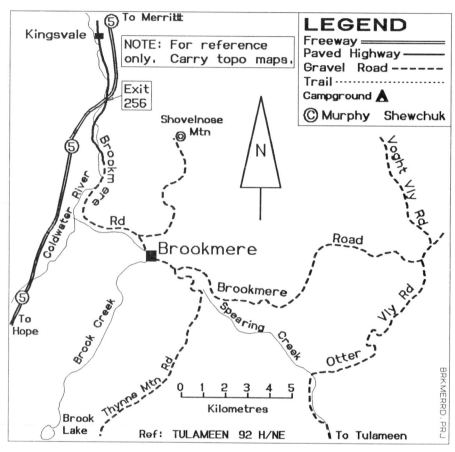

Map 6: Kingsvale / Brookmere / Thynne Mtn Area.

Exit 256 (Coldwater Road) is the departure point for both the Brookmere Road and the Coldwater Road. With the exit as km 0 reference, head south and you will cross two new bridges over the Coldwater River at km 1.5 and km 2.7. The 36K sign near km 3 refers to the distance to Merritt where most of the logs from this area are hauled.

Brookmere Road climbs steadily away from the Coldwater River after crossing the Kettle Valley Railway tracks near km 5. Moose Hill, one of the first steep climbs, has a much-deserved bad reputation for being treacherous in winter.

A side road at km 8.6 (just before the 42K marker) heads up the hill to the top of Shovelnose Mountain. There are a maze of forest roads on the mountainside, but access improvements for cellular telephone service may make the right road a little easier to find. It is about 9.3 km to the 1830 metre peak of Shovelnose Mountain, but the view from the top can be worth the effort.

The Brookmere water tank and caboose at km 10.2 mark the centre of the community. If you look carefully, you may see the foundation of a railway roundhouse and a large fuel storage tank, more reminders of the days when the railroad was the king of transportation.

B eyond the community, at km 11.5, a railway crossing marks the start of a Forest Service road to the top of Thynne Mountain. (See *Thynne Mountain Road* for details.) This is also the start of the Thynne Mountain snowmobile trail network. Various work crews have built a loading ramp and cleared a parking area near the old railway crossing.

The road to the left crosses the tracks (they may have been removed by the time you read this) and winds 15 km across the plateau, joining the Coalmont Road about 18 km south of Aspen Grove.

The road from Coquihalla Highway 5 to the junction south of Brookmere is kept open year around, but Thynne Mountain Road and the road from Brookmere to Coalmont Road are normally only passable in summer.

•••

Fig. 8: K.V.R. Water Tank at Brookmere.

Thynne Mountain Road

Statistics   **For map, see page 52.**

Distance:	23 km, Brookmere Road to Thynne Peak.
Travel Time:	Approximately one half hour.
Condition:	Gravel with rough sections.
Season:	July through October.
Topo Maps:	Aspen Grove 92H/15 (1:50,000).
	Tulameen 92H/10 (1:50,000).
Forest Maps:	Merritt - Princeton.
Communities:	Merritt & Hope.

Thynne Mountains is an easily accessible alpine ridge where plants and animals typical of the North Cascades can be seen. Countless western anemone blossom in the wake of the retreating snow, then thrust their "towhead baby" seed pods up to catch the wind. Avalanche lilies present their yellow blossoms to the sun, then shyly fade away for another summer. Colorful blue, pink and white phlox hug the ground to avoid the incessant breeze. Many other varieties of wildflowers, some of them stunted by the short summers, send forth their blossoms, then retreat into hiding.

Deer feed on the alpine growth during the short summer months while cattle graze on the lower slopes. Sheep also once roamed the alpine meadows. Bears enjoy the lush growth at the lower elevations and in the autumn can be sometimes seen reluctantly sharing the huckleberries with marmots and chipmunks.

The view from the top of Thynne Mountain encompasses the grassland plateau to the north and east, and the Coast Range and Cascade Mountains to the west and south. If the weather is clear, the ice-capped top of Mount Baker can be seen to the south through a "V" created by the Coquihalla Canyon.

Fig. 9: "Towhead Babies" on Thynne Mtn.

The rough gravel road to the top of the 2020-metre-high ancient volcanic peak services two microwave repeater sites and a B.C. Forest Service Fire Lookout. Two excellent fishing lakes are also nestled on the north side of the mountain only a short distance from the road (see Andys Lake Loop).

Considerable caution is necessary when travelling this road on weekdays as logging is taking place on the lower elevations of the mountain. The trucks usually start hauling very early in the morning, but usually make their last trip before 5:00 pm.

The kilometre signs used by the truck drivers can also help you through the maze of roads. The starting point, km 0, is at the railway crossing approximately 1.5 km southeast of Brookmere. The Thynne Mountain Road does not cross the tracks but keeps to the south, gradually climbing through the timber. Keep straight ahead at the Brook Creek Road junction at km 1.8 and to the right at a junction at a new log landing at km 4.8. Swing to the right at the Lower McPhail Road junction at km 6.8.

From this point, small red flags and yellow plastic tubes fastened high up trees and posts mark the route to the Unitel (CN-CP) microwave site at the top. Maintenance technicians find these flags particularly useful in winter when storms and deep snow obscures many of the usual landmarks.

You have two options at an important junction at km 10. If you take the Upper McPhail Road to the left, keeping right at the next two junctions, you will rejoin the Thynne Mtn Road near km 15 and avoid several loose, steep grades.

(If you keep right at Upper McPhail Road, at the junction at the 11-km sign take the lesser used road to the left. The road to the right heads into Andys Lake while the left road proceeds across a small flats and begins an undulating climb to the top.)

The Merritt Snowmobile Club has converted an old CN-CP generator building to a clubhouse at km 16 and, half a kilometre later, the steep, rough climb to the crest of the ridge begins. The road levels off at a microwave radio repeater site at km 17.5 and then follows the top of the ridge for approximately five kilometres to the CN-CP (Unitel) communications site.

There are several small, shallow lakes and ponds nestled in the folds of the alpine ridge. Wilderness camping options abound and the wildflower meadows can be quite spectacular in July and August.

●●●

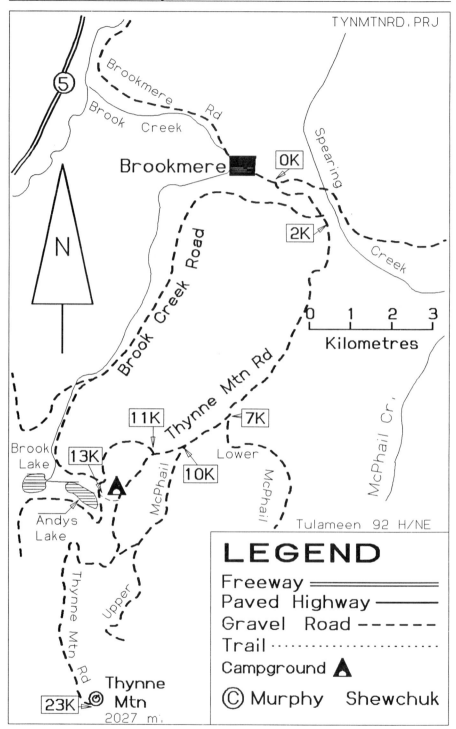

Map 7: Thynne Mtn Road / Andys Lake Loop.

Andys Lake Loop

Statistics   **For map, see page 52.**

Distance:	Approximately 18 km round trip.
Travel Time:	one half to one hour.
Condition:	Summer road, except by snowmobile.
Season:	Summer and Winter.
Topo Maps:	Aspen Grove 92 H/15 (1:50,000).
	Tulameen 92 H/10 (1:50,000).
Forest Maps:	Merritt - Princeton.
Communities:	Merritt & Hope.

Thynne Mountain, particularly the Andys Lake area, is of recreational interest both winter and summer. The only time of the year that the wildlife have the area much to themselves is in the spring when the mud and the mosquitoes keep the less-determined fishermen at home. Andys Lake is also a destination point on the snowmobile circuit that the Merritt Snowmobile Club has developed on Thynne Mountain.

Because the snowmobile route differs somewhat from the roads when winter logging is active, the following directions will apply primarily to summer traffic. Snowmobilers should check the maps posted at the starting point near Brookmere or obtain a copy of the snowmobile route map from the Forest Service in Merritt.

For the first 10 km, the directions are the same as for the Thynne Mountain Road. The starting point, km 0, is at the railway crossing approximately 1.5 km southeast of Brookmere. The Thynne Mountain Road does not cross the tracks but keeps to the south, gradually climbing through the timber. Keep straight ahead at the Brook Creek Road junction at km 1.8 and to the right at a junction at a new log landing at km 4.8. Swing to the right at the Lower McPhail Road junction at km 6.8.

Keep right at the Upper McPhail Road/Thynne Mountain Road junction at km 10 and again at the 11 km sign. The road to the right heads into Andys Lake while the Thynne road proceeds across a small flats and begins an undulating climb to the top.

Keep left at a little used road at km 12.1 and watch for a junction at 12.4 where the road to the right dips quickly down a short hill before disappearing around the corner. Remember this junction as it provides an alternate route out.

Fig. 10: Logging truck on Thynne Mtn Road.

Andys Lake North Recreation Site, at km 13, serves as a base for fishing and hiking in the area. Beyond the rec site, the road gradually descends to a creek crossing and another small rec site nearer the lake. A rough road named "Crosser" near km 13 links Andys Lake with Thynne Mtn Road. There are trails through the trees and a shelter near the northeast shore of Andys Lake.

From the junction at km 12.4, the loop continues north and then northeast as Brook Creek Road. Keep an eye out for a trail into Andys Lake less than half a kilometre farther along, and watch for a trail into Brook Lake. A major road comes in from the left about 3.4 km from the junction, and then its all downhill to Thynne Mountain Road, about three kilometres from Brookmere.

●●●

Coldwater Road

Statistics   **For maps, see pages 4 & 62.**

Distance:	31 km, Exit 256 to Highway 5A/97C at Merritt.
Travel Time:	One half hour.
Condition:	Paved.
Season:	Year around.
Topo Maps:	Tulameen 92 H/NE (1:100,000).
	Merritt 92 I/SE (1:100,000).
Forest Maps:	Merritt - Princeton.
Communities:	Merritt.

The original highway through the Coldwater Valley followed the benches above the river, well below Coquihalla Highway 5. When survey work started on the Coquihalla Highway, local ranchers and Natives objected to the destruction of the prime rangeland that would take place if the valley route was chosen for a multi-lane divided highway. Their voices were heeded and the new highway was routed along the mountainside, well away from agricultural land. With the southern access to the Coldwater Road (Exit 256) as km 0, the first diversion on this paved backroad is Kingsvale at km 2.7.

Kingsvale does not have a connection to royalty, but instead was named after Del King. King, son-in-law of Nicola Valley pioneer Jesus Garcia, settled on land where a railway station and post office where later located. High hopes for a long-term settlement here disappeared shortly after World War I when Major Goldman, then owner of the Nicola Ranch near Merritt, bought up the main ranching properties in the nearby Voght and Kane valleys. The railway underpass at Kingsvale marks the junction of a backroad west to Gillis and Murray lakes. (See Murray Lake Road for details.)

Fig. 11: Mule deer frequent the Coldwater Valley.

Kane Valley Road, at km 4, provides access to an excellent cross-country skiing area, a series of fine upland lakes, and, if time is no concern, a shortcut to Highway 5A/97C near Corbett Lake. (See Kane Valley Road for details.)

Patchett Road, at km 12.6, provides access to the upper reaches of Spius Creek and a convoluted backroad short-cut to Boston Bar. The shortcut to Boston Bar is difficult to find, even more difficult to describe, but it is an easy area in which to get lost.

The Coldwater Indian Reserve, at km 19, is home to well-known local Native artist, Phillip "Opie" Oppenheim. Opie has operated a studio and gallery here since 1987. His excellent work, in silver, jade and silkscreen prints, is much in demand.

Veale Road, near km 26, is the starting point of a gravel road that leads up to the top of 1693 metre high Iron Mountain and also to a fine fishing lake on the south slopes of the mountain. (See Gwen Lake Road for details.)

Thirty-one kilometres after leaving Exit 256, the Coldwater Road joins Highway 5A/97C, about two kilometres southeast of downtown Merritt.

●●●

Murray Lake Road

Statistics   **For map, see page 59.**

Distance:	33 km from Kingsvale to Juliet via Gillis and Murray lakes.
Travel Time:	One to two hours in dry weather.
Condition:	Gravel road with rough sections.
Season:	Mid-May through October.
Topo Maps:	Tulameen 92 H/NE (1:100,000). Yale 92 H/NW (1:100,000).
Forest Maps:	Merritt - Princeton.
Communities:	Merritt & Hope.

Gillis Lake, at the north end of this backroad, has an excellent Forest Service campsite and good trout fishing opportunities year around. The marshes at the southwest end of this boomerang-shaped lake can be quite productive early in the season. Although there are a few places to fish from shore, a canoe or cartop boat would be a useful accessory.

Murray Lake is a 2.5-km long, narrow lake lying in a north-south valley in the Cascades just west of the Coldwater River. It is a quiet, pretty lake suitable for canoeing or for fishing with a small boat and light tackle. There are small Forest Service campsites at both ends and a number of summer cottages on the east shore.

The southern access is from the Juliet exit on Coquihalla Highway 5, once a water stop on the Kettle Valley Railway. The road from Juliet is rough and climbs steeply for about five kilometres before reaching the south end of Murray Lake.

The northern access from Kingsvale, another old Kettle Valley Railway water stop, is in better condition because of logging traffic. To reach Kingsvale, take Exit 256 on Coquihalla

Highway 5 south of Merritt and drive north for 2.7 km to where the Coldwater Road passes under the railway track (30 km south of Merritt on the Coldwater Road).

Fig. 12: Murray Lake, looking south.

Murray Lake Road begins at the underpass so proceed straight west at the Kingsvale junction. Cross the Coldwater River at km 0.2 and swing south (left) on the road that begins climbing immediately. The road climbs steadily, switch-backing up the mountainside to Gillis Lake at km 5.0. There are a few hidden spots to park a vehicle or pitch a tent on the west shore of the lake, but the main recreation site is below the road on the north shore of Gillis Lake. The unmarked entrance to the Gillis Lake Forest Service Rec site is near the west end of the lake at km 6.4.

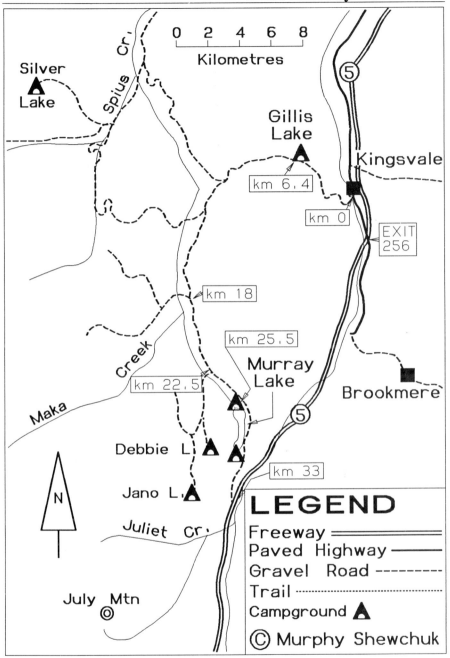

Map 8: Murray Lake Road.

Fig. 13: Bunchberry (Cornus canadensis) blossoms.

The Murray Lake Road then parallels a 500 kV power line to km 10 before swinging south and up Maka Creek. A junction at km 18 marks the Lower Maka Forest Service Road, keep left to Murray Lake. In this area, the road passes through second growth forest and large stands of aspen. Deer and bear are a frequent sight, especially in the evening and early morning. Keep left again at the Debbie Lake Forest Service Road junction near km 22.5. The road to the right heads into an active logging area and several small lakes.

At a junction near the 25-km signpost, the road swings right to Murray Lake while the road to the left continues to another logging operation. The Murray Lake North Forest Service rec site near km 25.5 is a large, open site with a day-use area and a place to launch a cartop boat. The islands in the lake provide shelter and fishing privacy from the limited traffic that passes this way.

The road past the cottages on the east shore of the lake appears to be designed to discourage traffic. It is rough, dusty and narrow and best approached with caution. The recreation site at the south end of Murray Lake is small with a little more shelter.

South of Murray Lake, the narrow, rough gravel road edges across the mountainside for three kilometres before making a two-kilometre switch-back descent to Coquihalla Highway 5 at Juliet.

●●●

Kane Valley Road

Statistics   **For map, see page 62.**

Distance: 35 km from Coquihalla Hwy to Highway 5A/97C.
Travel Time: One to two hours in dry weather.
Condition: Gravel road with rough sections.
Season: Anytime except spring break-up.
Topo Maps: Merritt 92 I/2 (1:50,000).
                 Aspen Grove 92 H/15 (1:50,000).
Forest Maps: Merritt - Princeton.
Communities: Merritt.

Kane Valley Road is a back country thoroughfare, less than three hours from the Lower Mainland, that offers three-season enjoyment for almost any outdoor interest.

The three-season part deserves a bit more elaboration. Unlike the "dry weather only" recommendation I usually hang on the more remote backroads, this route really should be avoided only during late March and April, a season known as spring break-up.

Those of you who aren't familiar with the term "spring break-up" as it applies to this part of the B.C. Interior should think of it as the time of the year when everything turns to mush. The ice breaks-up on the lakes, turning the frozen surface to mush and trapping a few unwary snowmobilers and ice fishermen each year. The gravel roads break-up, revealing a base of bottomless red clay mixed with a few oilpan-eating boulders. Cross-country skis break-up when their owners collide with a dislodged boulder or patch of bare ground. Drivers have been known to suffer mental breakdown when they discover that they are stuck up to their axles in the middle of an otherwise normal road, but that's another subject.

Spring excluded, there are three seasons and several reasons to explore this east-west lying valley in the mountains south of Merritt.

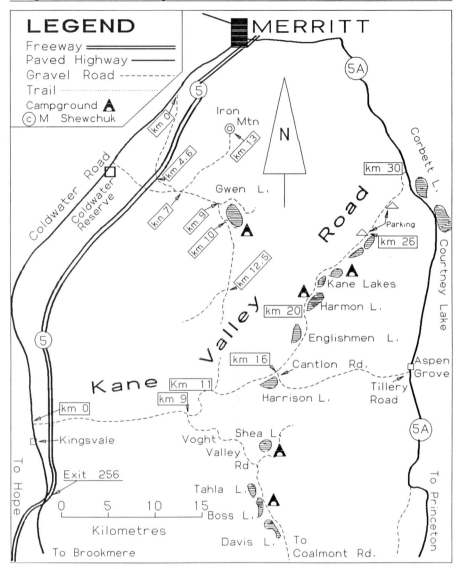

Map 9: Iron Mountain / Kane Valley Area.

My wife, the cross-country skiing fanatic, will obviously tell you that the best season is winter and the best reason is the 40 kilometres of well-marked cross-country ski trails. She should know, because she helped promote them way back when cross-country skiers used wooden skis and bamboo poles. I certainly won't argue with her, I have enough trouble keeping up without trying to talk and breathe at the same time.

My neighbor, the fisherman, was a little peeved when they poisoned off most of the lakes a while back, but now that fishing is back better than normal, he thinks the early summer and fall seasons are the best. Mind you, he's like me in not being able to understand people who sit by a hole in the ice and try to entice a trout to swallow a kernel of corn on the end of a fishing line. Hot rum and a crackling fireplace seem to both of us to be better surroundings if one wants to sit still in winter.

I think I've digressed a little from the original intention to expound upon a new and worthy backroad adventure for you to undertake. Blame it on the fact that the cool weather affects the brain cells—I'll put my hat on and get back to serious business.

The Kane Valley Road has two ends, unlike some of the roads we have covered and it has the same name at both ends (ditto). Most of the cross-country skiing traffic approaches it from the east off of what is now Highway 5A/97C, 18 km south of Merritt and two kilometres north of the world famous Corbett Lake Country Inn. (Please excuse this blatant commercialism, but owner Peter McVey is a chef whose cooking, fly-tieing and rod-making is world-famous.)

Because we both know that the odds are that you will be driving up the Coquihalla Highway from Hope and that you will have a four-wheel drive vehicle or a decent set of tire chains, I will outline your route from the west end, near the old Kettle Valley Railway community of Kingsvale. As this end of the Kane Valley Road isn't first on the snow plow priority list, snow tires and chains aren't an idle suggestion.

To get to the west end of the Kane Valley Road, take Exit 256 off the Coquihalla Highway, approximately 80 km north of Hope or 30 km south of Merritt. Continue north down the Coldwater River valley (south will get you to Brookmere and a dead end in winter) through a railway underpass at Kingsvale and up the hill to the junction of the Coldwater Road and Kane Valley Road, about 3.5 km from the freeway interchange.

Swing right at the junction and follow the road as it climbs steadily eastward up Voght Creek, passing under the freeway at km 1 and through scrub pine and aspen to km 5.

Voght deserves more than a passing mention, for William Henry Voght was the Father of the City of Merritt. He was born in 1832 in Holstein, now part of West Germany, and came to North America as a teenager. After temporary stays in Iowa, New Orleans and the California Gold Rush, he joined a group headed for the Fraser River Gold Rush in 1858. After two seasons of chasing the elusive yellow metal, young Bill Voght took up farming across the Fraser River from Boston Bar. He farmed there for 13 years before moving in 1873 to where Merritt stands today. When coal was discovered in the nearby hills, Voght promoted the construction of a railway into the valley and surveyed the new coal mining community on part of his farm. After a short illness, Voght died in February, 1911, less than two months before the City of Merritt received its charter. The Voght Valley connection comes from William Henry Voght's eldest son, also named William, who settled here in the late 1880s.

The Kane Valley Road, gravel, twisting and narrow in places, levels off somewhat near km 5 and parallels the creekbed through some excellent moose pasture. Merritt's Tolko Industries is selective logging throughout much of the valley and its efforts are clearly visible here.

A lone log house in the field to the south of the road near km 8 is believed to have been built by John Smith when he settled in the valley in the late 1880s. His wife, Jessie Ann, details the difficulties of their homesteading life in Widow Smith of Spence's Bridge (Sonotek® Publishing, 1989). They lived here for 10 years before moving to Spences Bridge in 1897.

Approximately one kilometre farther along, a junction and sign marks the road to Boss, Davis, Tahla and Shea lakes. Known as Voght Valley Road, this 15-km-long backroad was once part of the trail from the Nicola Valley to the mines at Granite Creek. Today, recreationists find Voght Valley of particular interest for the lakes and the Forest Service recreation sites at each one. Voght Valley Road joins the Coalmont Road about 20 km south of Aspen Grove.

Keep straight ahead at the junction as the Kane Valley Road passes through Voght Valley Ranch and begins to swing northeast up Kanevale Creek. Cantlon Road, another side road just past man-made Harrison Lake, winds 10 kilometres easterly through the upland timber to Highway 5A, coming out as Tillery Road just south of Aspen Grove. It is a pleasant drive in the autumn, but is rough and narrow in places.

As much of the log hauling is done to Highway 5A, the roadside numbers begin a countdown near the Voght Valley Ranch. The Cantlon/Tillery Road junction is about 16 km from Kingsvale and at the 14K roadside marker. Englishmen Lake is the next point-of-interest along the route. Like most of the lakes in the valley, it has been dammed to increase storage capacity for agriculture irrigation. Also like most of the lakes in the valley, it was purged to remove coarse fish several years ago. Check the current fishing regulations as restrictions do apply.

Fig. 14: Photographing columbine in the Kane Valley.

Harmon Lake at km 20 [10K] is the best known and busiest of the Kane Lakes chain. A large open Forest Service recreation site here is seldom empty except in the dead of winter when the only access is snowmobile, ski or snowshoe. A trail with a series of information plaques winds through a demonstration forest on the southeast side of the lake.

Harmon Lake marks the west end of the Kane Valley cross-country ski trail system. This network extends to the ridges on both sides of the valley and along the valley to the 2K signpost with several maintained parking lots and rest areas.

A sign marks Lower Kane Lake near km 21. At the time of writing this lake was a catch and release fishery with a gasoline motor prohibition. Before the restrictions went into effect, I watched a smiling grey-haired lady pull in a beautiful rainbow trout that must have been close to two kilograms (five pounds) after half-a-dozen casts with light fly-fishing tackle. Upper Kane Lake is a few minutes farther along the road.

A ski trail named "Overeasy" (a blatant lie) near the junction of Upper and Lower Second Lakes marks one of the many ski trails that wind up to the ridge on the north side of the valley. (See the map on page 68 for details.) With the help of local volunteers, work grant programs and the Forest Service, the extensive network of trails on both sides of the valley from Harmon Lake to Highway 5A has been well-maintained during the past several winters. Work was undertaken in the summer of 1989 to widen a few of the trails that suffered from shading by the trees. One of the warming shelters was also moved to a sunnier location. Fortunately the Forest Service has posted maps at several locations making ski exploring a lot easier than it was a decade ago.

The 30-kilometre-long Kane Valley Road climbs steadily from Kingsvale, reaching an elevation of about 1220 metres (4,000 feet) before dropping rather quickly in the last two kilometres to Highway 5A near Corbett Lake. Along the way it passes several excellent fishing lakes and a network of cross-country ski trails noted for their long season and dry powder conditions. Snow depths seldom exceed one metre (three feet), but skiing has often been good from mid-December to mid-March.

If you are looking for some mid-winter backroads exploring, give it a try. But don't forget your skis *and* your tire chains. If you must wait for spring, bring your boat and your gumboots.

●●●

Kane Valley X-C Ski Area

Statistics	For maps, see pages 62 & 68.
Distance:	Approximately 42 km of marked trails.
Travel Time:	Not applicable.
Condition:	Trails are marked and groomed regularly.
Season:	Mid-December to mid-March.
Topo Maps:	Merritt 92 I/2 (1:50,000).
	Aspen Grove 92 H/15 (1:50,000).
Forest Maps:	Merritt - Princeton.
Communities:	Merritt.

When snow covers everything in a white blanket, the chain of lakes along the floor of the Kane Valley, south of Merritt, become a haven for ice fishermen and cross-country skiers.

The Kane Valley ski trails, twenty minutes south of Merritt and an hour north of Princeton, are only a few minutes drive off Highway 5A/97C, north of Corbett Lake. Lying on a tangent between Highway 5A/97C and Coquihalla Highway 5 and at a base elevation of 1160 metres (3800 feet) the valley has a micro-climate that can provide ideal cross-country ski conditions. The snow is generally dry, although seldom more than 1 to 1.5 metres deep, and the air temperatures are around -5 to -15 degrees Celsius throughout the winter. In fact, during the 1984-85 season, skiing varied from good to excellent for most of the period between Halloween and Easter.

The best winter access to the ski area is via the Kane Valley Road from Highway 5A/97C near Corbett Lake, 17 km south of Merritt. The Ministry of Highways maintains several parking areas at points where the ski trails cross the Kane Valley Road. The first is a wide section approximately two kilometres from Highway

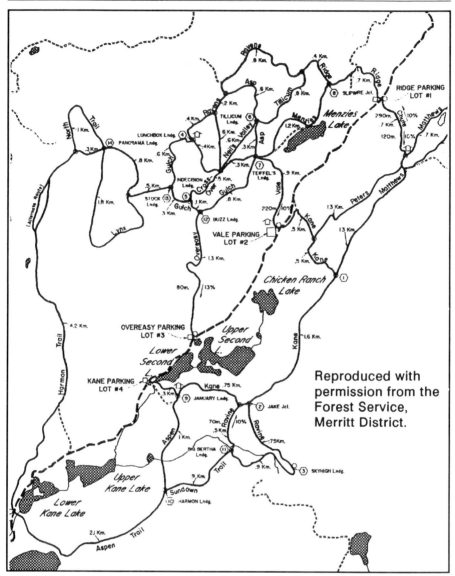

Map 10: Kane Valley Cross-Country Ski Area.
Full size maps are posted on site or available from the Forest Service.

5A/97C. The second parking lot is the largest, with room to turn a bus around and a shelter near the road. The third or fourth parking areas also provide good access to the trails.

Up-to-date maps are usually posted at trail register boards a short distance off of the road near the parking lots. Maps are also available from the Ministry of Forests, Bag 4400, Merritt, B.C. V0K 2B0 or, preferably, in person from their office at 2196 Quilchena Avenue, Merritt, (8:30 to 16:30 weekdays). These maps provide detailed information on the Kane Valley trails, including length, level of difficulty and location of shelters.

Trail conditions vary, depending on snowfall and maintenance, and maintenance is subject to the availabilty of funding. However, let me make a few suggestions. If you are out for an easy ski with young or new skiers, try the Kane Trail from the second parking lot. It has a bit of a steep start, but from then on it climbs steadily for several kilometres with a few twists and dips to add some challenge. If you wish, you can leave a second vehicle near a footbridge at the west end of the trail at Lower Second Lake, and enjoy the slightly steeper downhill run to a shelter near the lake and then through the trees to the road.

The Harmon Trail can also be accessed from the second parking lot for a full loop that totals about 16 kilometres. It climbs up Vale initially, and then continues to climb up the north side of the valley as the Gulch Trail and Harmon Trail before making a long run down an old logging road to Harmon Lake. You can cross Kane Valley Road here and after skirting Harmon Lake, climb east and up the south side of the valley on the Aspen Trail. The Sundown and Ravine trails will allow you to keep high on the south slopes of the valley, or you can follow Aspen down to a shelter at January Landing where there is often a campfire going. The section of trail from the Sundown junction to January Landing has a long, steep hill that will give you a thrill or a chill, depending on your skiing abilities. If you aren't equipped for narrow, steep trails, an alternate route was recently cut through the timber in this area. From January Landing, you can follow the Kane Trail back to Kane Valley Road and the second parking lot. Some sections of this route are fairly steep and will require good climbing and descending skills, although they wouldn't qualify as expert telemark slopes.

Accomodations in the Merritt area are plentiful, although reservations may be required. Tourism British Columbia's accomodation guide provides a full listing and additional information may be available from the Merritt Chamber of Commerce, Box 1649, Merritt, B.C. V0K 2B0. Telephone (604) 378-5634.

●●●

Fig. 15: On the Ravine Trail.

Gwen Lake Road

(Iron Mountain)

Statistics	For map, see page 62.
Distance:	14 km, Coldwater Road to Iron Mtn Summit.
	11 km, Coldwater Road to Gwen Lake.
Travel Time:	One half hour.
Condition:	Gravel, some rough sections.
Season:	May through October.
Topo Maps:	Merritt 92 I/2 (1:50,000).
	Aspen Grove 92 H/15 (1:50,000).
Forest Maps:	Merritt - Princeton.
Communities:	Merritt.

Iron Mountain was the site of considerable mining exploration in the latter part of the nineteenth and early part of the twentieth centuries. George M. Dawson, the noted geologist, first used the Iron Mountain name in his Geological Survey of Canada Report of 1877-78. The British Columbia Minister of Mines report for 1896 indicates that twenty-four mineral claims had been staked on Iron Mountain that year. In addition to iron, also present was gold, silver and copper, but little came of the prospects.

In 1927, Emmett Todd, a veteran prospector, discovered a silver-lead vein one kilometre south of the summit that showed considerable promise. A shaft was sunk more that 30 metres deep on the Leadville claim before a fault was encountered and the vein was lost. In 1947, the shaft was reopened as the Lucky Todd Mine and 32 tonnes of ore were shipped to the Trail smelter, containing 2000 grams of silver, 5360 kilograms of lead, and 220 kilograms of zinc.

The effort was shortlived, however, and except for prospectors and rockhounds searching the old waste dumps for traces of jasper, peacock copper and malachite, Iron Mountain has remained quiet.

Gwen Lake Road (Veale Road at this point) swings east from the Coldwater Road about five kilometres south of Highway 5A/97C. With the Coldwater Road—Veale Road junction as km 0, follow Veale Road up the hillside through hay fields at km 0.9 and 2.2 and under the Coquihalla Highway at km 4.6. Keep left at the Comstock Road junction at km 6.2.

Comstock Road joins Coquihalla Highway 5 at Exit 276, about 1.5 km to the west (down the hill). It then continues down the mountain to the Coldwater Indian Reserve village.

A junction about 7.0 km from the Coldwater Road marks the turnoff to Iron Mountain, with the summit six kilometres to the north and Gwen Lake four kilometres to the east.

At the 6.5 marker, approximately four kilometres up Iron Mountain, a very rough road leads to the left (west). It winds through the open timber for about 1.3 kilometres before reaching the site of an old mine shaft. You may find some interesting ore samples near the shaft and where the mountain top has been trenched.

Iron Mountain is a maze of communications buildings and antennas with more being added at the time of writing, but despite this, the 1693-metre peak offers an excellent view of Sugarloaf Mountain and the Nicola Valley grasslands.

Back at the junction at km 7.0, the road to the southeast continues toward Gwen Lake. The first road to the left provides access to an Indian Reserve and ranch. The one kilometre access road to the Gwen Lake Forest Service recreation site branches to the left near km 10. This road is very rough with boulders lurking in the mud holes, ready to jump out at your oil pan.

Beyond the Gwen Lake junction, the main road continues through the uplands, eventually following Howarth Creek down to the Kane Valley Road about 11 km east of the Coldwater Road. The section between Gwen Lake and the Kane Valley Road is a real maze that should not be attempted without a good topographic map, a compass, a full fuel tank and plenty of time. If you do decide to try it, keep left at a junction near km 2.5 and follow the road across the 500 kV powerline at km 3.7. Keep right at a junction in a clearing near km 5 and again at an old junction near km 7.7. If you make all the right moves, you should reach Kane Valley Road about 11 km from the Gwen Lake junction and 11 km from the Coldwater Road.

•••

Princeton to Merritt

(Highway 5A)

Statistics   **For map, see page 4.**

Distance:	Princeton – Merritt 89 km.
Travel Time:	One hour.
Conditions:	Paved throughout.
Topo Maps:	Princeton, B.C. 92 H/SE (1:100,000).
	Tulameen, B.C. 92 H/NE (1:100,000).
	Merritt, B.C. 92 I/SE (1:100,000).
Forest Maps:	Merritt - Princeton.
Communities:	Princeton - Aspen Grove - Merritt.

Princeton lies 289 km east of Vancouver, at the junction of Highways 3 and 5A, on the Crowsnest Route. Princeton, originally called Vermilion Forks, has long been a mining community. The native Indians mined the nearby red ochre deposits to make paint for trade with the coastal tribes. With the gold rush of the 1860s, Princeton became the gateway to the Boundary District. Coal was soon discovered beneath the streets of the town; then copper became the source of revenue. Similko Mines, south of Princeton, continues to work a portion of the rich copper belt that extends from Chelan, Washington, to Cache Creek, B. C.

At the outskirts of lower Princeton, the inscription on a large granite block reads:
MILE ZERO No. 5 HIGHWAY
AUGUST 22, 1967.
PRINCETON, B.C.
A short distance north of the Mile Zero marker, Highway 5A crosses the Tulameen River then passes a junction to the left. The

Tulameen Road leads northwest, following the Tulameen River upstream through Coalmont and Tulameen to Otter Lake. Otter Lake Provincial Park, a 45 unit campground on a delta in the lake, is located 33 km from Princeton. Along the shores of Otter Lake, the pavement changes to a good gravel road, continuing northward to rejoin Highway 5A near Aspen Grove. Along the way it also has a change in identity, although I have never been able to determine exactly where. At Princeton it is signed Tulameen Road and at Aspen Grove the signpost reads Coalmont Road.

From Princeton north to the Missezula Lake junction, Highway 5A winds across rolling benchland covered with bunchgrass, stands of lodgepole pine and the occasional long-needled ponderosa pine. The glacial deposits are a mass of yellow each spring with the sunflower-like blossoms of arrowleaf balsamroot. To the east is Sagebrush Downs, the community racetrack and fair facilities. Further east, you will see the line of the former Kettle Valley Railway (now C.P.R.) as it winds up the hillside on its way to Summerland.

A junction nine kilometres north of Princeton marks the start of a gravel road that leads 32 km north to long, narrow Missezula Lake. Also at this point, Highway 5 leaves the grasslands and begins a steady climb through the narrow Allison Valley. It briefly opens into hay fields and picturesque Allison Creek, complete with beaver dams and yellow water lilies.

The Allison Creek fish barrier at km 16.9 marks the start of a chain of small lakes and reed-covered ponds that extend most of the way to Merritt. Fishermen and ducks are plentiful on these lakes. Deer are also so plentiful as to be a road hazard in the evenings. It's not uncommon to see the eyes of a dozen or more deer peering at you as you drive by after dusk. It is also not uncommon to have to brake to avoid hitting them as they wander across the highway.

On one rather cold, damp November day, I had the experience of a lifetime near here. I was travelling south from Merritt to Keremeos when I came over the crest of a hill and saw a gray lump on the road in my lane. Something bothered me, so I stood on the brakes and slid to a halt a few metres from the object. It turned out to be a very large, cold and stunned loon. Loons are helpless out of water, and this one must have assumed that the icy wet road was water. Now it couldn't move.

I took my old jacket and carefully wrapped the big bird, placing it in a cardboard box on the back seat of the car. Destination: open water. There wasn't any before Princeton, so we decided on the pools at Bromley Rock on the Similkameen River.

74

Unfortunately, the loon wasn't keen on waiting. The warmth of the jacket and the car revived the bird and it made a noisy attempt to get out of the box. The next half hour varied between comic and panic as we tried to keep the powerful bill from creating havoc while still keeping our vehicle on the busy highway.

At Bromley Rock, I carefully unwrapped the now fully revived loon and gently lowered it into the water. It skittered two metres out on the pool, stopped and turned to look at us, called its haunting call, then bobbed downstream as though nothing had happened.

Fig. 16: On the mountainside above Allison Lake.

Allison Lake Provincial Park, at km 28.6, is divided by Highway 5A. Above the road is the campground, while below the road is a boat launch, picnic tables and beach. Many of the camping units of this small park overlook the lake with a thicket of Douglas fir absorbing the traffic noise of the nearby highway.

In the mid-1960's, my family and I spent a two week vacation based at the Sky Blue Lodge at the north end of Allison Lake. The lodge and cabins have long since disappeared and are being replaced by a cottage subdivision. If you are interested in exploring, a four-wheel-drive road to the east of Allison Lake will take you up to Stringer Lake. A few minutes north of Allison Lake a two-kilometre-long long hill climbs up onto the plateau country.

Hornet Lakes Road, a gravel forestry road to the right near the KM 35 signpost, climbs steeply up Missezula Mountain. This is the beginning of a network of old logging roads that are best explored with a four-wheel-drive vehicle, Forest Service and topographic maps, a good compass and lots of time. With care, you can follow the maze north past a series of potholes to Highway 5A at km 48. Watch for logging trucks.

Another junction, at km 37, marks a backroad to the AP Ranch resort and the Gulliford Lakes area. The Forest Service maintains a dozen recreation sites on a group of lakes lying west of the highway. A gravel road links Highway 5A with the Otter Valley Road (also known as Coalmont Road) via the Gulliford Lakes group. In addition to the fishing and camping opportunities of the area, there is also some challenging backroads exploring as well. The AP Ranch junction also marks the southern border of the grasslands of the Nicola Valley cattle country. To the north, the vista is one of aspen and pine dotted hillsides, bunchgrass, Hereford cattle, ducks and the occasional moose.

Duck-covered ponds on either side of the highway and a cattle guard are all that mark the junction of Dillard Creek Road at km 48. Missezula Lake is 10 km southeast and fishing, canoeing and cool-water swimming await you. Watch for logging trucks and check the ruts and boulders before taking a heavy trailer down to the Forest Service recreation site at the north end of the lake.

Otter Lake Provincial Park is 43 km south of the Highway 5A and Coalmont Road junction at km 54.5. Coalmont Road (also known as the Otter Valley Road) rejoins Highway 5A in Princeton. Side trips along it include the historic Granite Creek gold and platinum placer diggings near Coalmont, and a backroad that runs from downtown Tulameen over the mountains to Coquihalla Highway 5 near the toll booths. (See the *Coquihalla— Tulameen Road* for details.)

Bates Road, one kilometre farther north, leads to Kentucky-Alleyne Provincial Park. A score of fine upland lakes lie at the end of the six kilometre drive to the northeast. Two round ponds separate Kentucky and Alleyne lakes. In high water, these can provide swimming as well as canoeing and fishing. B.C. Parks has a 61-unit campground with good walking trails around the lakes.

Aspen Grove, at km 60.7, can be your place to stock up on gasoline, groceries and your fishing licence before heading for the hills—or the lakes.

A major junction at km 62.8 marks the Okanagan Connector (Hwy 97C). Phase III of the Coquihalla Highway system, this 90-km-long four-lane divided highway shortens the drive from Merritt to Kelowna by three hours. It has to climb to do it, though. At the high point of the highway, it reaches an elevation of 1728 metres, before making a 32 km run down to Westbank.

Corbett Lake Country Inn's Peter McVey (km 70) has developed an excellent reputation as a gourmet cook and fly fisherman. McVey trained in the kitchens of the Lord Mayor of London and worked in a number of large hotels before settling down to the quieter life at Corbett Lake.

Local skiers, in cooperation with the Forest Service, have developed over 42 km of groomed cross-country ski trails in the Kane Valley area west of Corbett Lake (km 72). The trails are well marked with four separate parking areas. Maps are posted at the parking lots and check-in stations. (See *Kane Valley Road* and *Kane Valley X-C Ski Area* for more information.)

Fig. 17: Lundbom Lake.

I ron Mountain Road, at km 73, winds up into private ranchland on the eastern slopes of Iron Mountain. Logan's Marsh, across Highway 5A from Iron Mountain Road, is an excellent wetland reclamation project undertaken jointly by Ducks Unlimited Canada and the Quilchena Cattle Company.

Lundbom Lake, four kilometres east of Highway 5A at km 77, lies in the upland grassland with open range on three sides and forest cover on the fourth. There are Forest Service campsites at both ends of the two-kilometre-long lake and plenty of roads and trails to explore.

A beaver pond a short distance north of the Lundbom Lake junction marks the crest of the long descent to Coquihalla Highway 5 and Merritt. This was a 10 per cent grade before the road was reconstructed. If you are driving or pulling a heavy rig, this is still a good place to check your hitch and your brakes. The road descends almost 480 metres (1570 ft) in the next seven kilometres.

A junction to the left just past the pond (km 80) provides access to the Old Nicola Road, a 10-km-long narrow, sidehill short-cut to the foot of Nicola Lake. This is no route for big-rigs or the weak-hearted traveller. This is the original 1870s wagon road from the village of Nicola to the mines at Granite Creek and it hasn't seen much improvement since then.

The Coquihalla Highway 5 Interchange (Exit 286), at the bottom the hill, is marked with a traffic light. The red-roofed log building nearby is the area travel information centre—one of the finest in the BC Interior. In addition to racks of brochures and maps, the info centre has forestry displays and a small gift shop where local books and souvenir items can be purchased. The Godey Creek Trail network behind the centre is well worth exploring.

The interchange will require a decision. Straight ahead takes you past the Coldwater Road junction and into Merritt. A right turn and you are on your way to Kamloops or Nicola Lake while a left turn takes you south on Coquihalla Highway 5 to Hope and points west.

If you've come up from the Coast and are looking for an alternate route back to Hope, you might consider taking the Coldwater Road as far south as the interchange south of Kingsvale (Exit 256). This route is paved most of the way, with a few interesting diversions including native artist "Opie" Oppenheim's studio at the Coldwater village. "Opie's" original silkscreen paintings have an unique style that has garnered him considerable favorable attention.

The traffic lights at the corner of Nicola Avenue and Voght Street in downtown Merritt mark another important junction. Straight ahead and Highway 8 will take you to Spences Bridge and the Trans-Canada Highway. Turn to the right and you will continue on Highway 5A past another chain of lakes to Kamloops and the Trans-Canada Highway. Why not stay a day or two while you decide on your next destination?

●●●

Kentucky-Alleyne Prov. Park

Statistics	For map, see page 81.
Distance:	6 km, Highway 5A to Kentucky-Alleyne Park. 8 km to north end of Alleyne Lake.
Travel Time:	10 minutes.
Condition:	Paved throughout.
Season:	Year around.
Topo Maps:	Aspen Grove 92 H/15 (1:50,000).
Forest Maps:	Merritt - Princeton.
Communities:	Merritt, Aspen Grove & Princeton.

Katharine paddled at the bow of the yellow canoe. Madeleine sat in the centre leaning up against the carrying yoke. I sat at the stern, paddle in hand, but camera at the ready as we drifted toward the reeds at the north end of Alleyne Lake, intent on capturing a marsh wren nest on film. We were enjoying the late spring afternoon sun, oblivious to growling stomachs and the aromatic scent of supper cooking on the campfire that drifted lazily over the water.

As the reeds parted on a muskrat waterway, Katharine stopped, pointing to a nondescript mound on the water's edge. I strained to see what had caught her attention and gradually made out the near-perfect camouflage of a nest. I quietly put down the paddle and focused the telephoto lens on the red eye of a loon.

Katharine held the canoe steady and Madeleine sat motionless only a metre or two from the big bird. The sound of the shutter was all that could be heard, but it was enough to disturb the nervous loon. As we backed away from the nest, it clumsily pushed its muscular chest over the bed of reeds and slid deep into the water. We had only moved a few metres when it surfaced, almost within reach of the canoe, and began a dance guaranteed to frighten all but the most determined of predators. While Katharine carefully guided us away from the loon's nest, I continued to photograph the splashing loon as it screamed and threatened us. Water flew everywhere. Twice it feigned an attack before retreating and again throwing a spray of water in our direction.

As I ran out of film, we slipped clear of the loon's territory and the adrenalin levels in all four of us began to subside.

Two-kilometre-long Alleyne Lake lies south of Merritt, in the heart of the Nicola Valley cattle country. It is part of the Kentucky-Alleyne Provincial Park, established by Order-in-Council on March 5, 1981, under the jurisdiction of the Ministry of Lands, Parks and Housing. The Kentucky-Alleyne Park sign at Bates Road, on Highway 5A about 5.3 kilometres south of Aspen Grove, gives no hint of the multitude of fine upland lakes that lie six kilometres to the east in this plateau region. Alleyne and Kentucky lakes are the largest, with a busy provincial government campground nestled in the timber between the two lakes.

Although not presently part of the park, there is also a rustic Forest Service Recreation Site at Bluey Lake. The access road to Bluey Lake winds south from Bates Road, starting to the right just before the park entrance sign at km 5.0. The rough gravel road passes through an old log cut and alongside an ancient canyon— probably a major river at the end of the last ice age. At the time of writing there was a very rough steep section at km 2.5 that would discourage all but the most ardent four-wheeler.

Local fishermen have long recognized the potential of the Kentucky-Alleyne area. In 1940, a map reserve was established for grazing, camping and fishing over one of the lots comprising the present Recreation Area. A second lot was temporarily added to the reserve in 1959, but was returned to grazing and reestablished in 1964. The 1981 O.I.C. established the multi-use concept of recreation and ranching, maintaining a low-profile park status on the area surrounding the junction of the two lakes.

Alleyne Lake, at 55 hectares (135 acres) in area, is the larger of the two main lakes while Kentucky Lake, at 44 hectares (108 acres), follows a close second. Bluey Lake covers an area of 28 hectares (70 acres). None of the lakes have natural spawning streams and instead must rely on the continuous stocking program undertaken by the Fish and Wildlife Branch. Alleyne Lake was rehabilitated in 1956 and Kentucky Lake in 1959 to remove an excess population of sculpin and suckers.

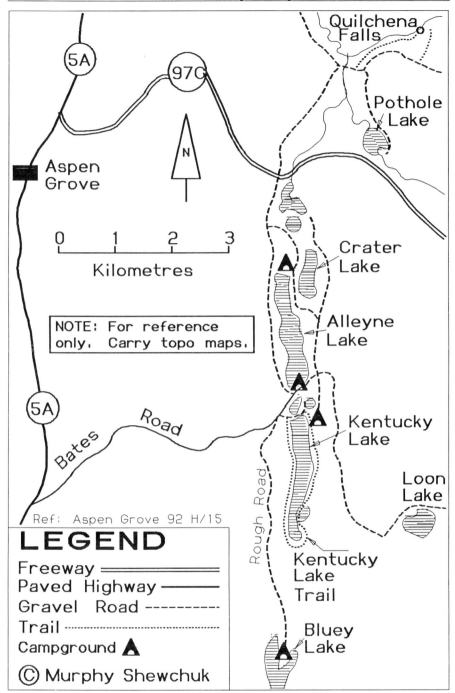

Map 11: Kentucky-Alleyne Provincial Park.

Kentucky and Alleyne lakes are a classic example of over-fishing. Most of the trout stocked each spring are caught before they have been in the lake a full year. Despite plenty of feed, including freshwater shrimp and chironomids, the average trout caught runs at 0.2 to 0.4 kilograms (1/2 to 3/4 pounds) although I once watched a young girl pull in a rainbow weighing two kilograms (4.5 pounds) from one of the ponds lying between Kentucky and Alleyne lakes.

Fig. 18: Fishermen on Kentucky Lake.

Loons also do their share of fishing. More than one fisherman has pulled in a rainbow with telltale marks that indicate it barely escaped the grip of a deep-diving loon.

The land is a classic example of glaciated topography with the numerous lakes and ponds set out in a north-south string. Alleyne Lake is located in the transition zone between the dry grasslands and the sightly wetter pine and fir forest. Scattered ponderosa pine and interior Douglas fir cover the western slopes near the lake while bunchgrass dominate the northern and eastern slopes. Kentucky and Bluey lakes are surrounded by pine and fir.

Several old roads encircle Alleyne Lake. They cross deeded land belonging to the Douglas Lake Cattle Company north and east of the lake and have been posted with "No Trespassing" signs to discourage the indiscriminate use of the delicate rangeland.

When I interviewed manager, Joe Gardiner, on the subject of access to the east side of Alleyne Lake, Crater Lake and Quilchena Falls, he indicated that Douglas Lake Ranch requires that hikers obtain permission before venturing on ranch property. This can be obtained by telephoning the ranch office at Douglas Lake at 350-3344 during normal business hours.

Youngsters particularly appreciate the marshes and hidden ponds along the route around Alleyne Lake. You can follow the gravel road northeast of the campground at the junction of Alleyne and Kentucky lakes, swinging north at the first side road. Carefully climb through the wooden gate and follow the tracks north along the ridge separating Alleyne and Crater lakes. The old cart tracks gradually swing to the west side of the valley and you can then return via the gravel road through the pine on the west side of Alleyne Lake.

Quilchena Falls has proven to be one of the more elusive attractions of the Douglas Plateau. It is well hidden among the scrub timber and sheltered in a canyon cut into the plateau. The maze of roads and cattle trails in the vicinity make it easy to miss. Its main attraction is that in May and June, when the runoff is at its peak, Quilchena Falls is one of the more spectacular waterfalls in the plateau region. Around the turn of the century, Quilchena Falls was seriously considered as a source of hydro electric power for the proposed mines of the Aspen Grove area.

If you are interested in a day-long round trip of about 15 kilometres, park your vehicle near the ponds at the junction of Kentucky and Alleyne lakes. Then follow the rough gravel road north along the west side of Alleyne Lake, through the locked gate and over the rangeland and through a tunnel under Hwy 97C for a total of about 6.5 kilometres. Take the right fork in the road at this point and cross Pothole Creek.

After crossing the creek, swing left into what was once a sawmill site or log yard. Cross the clearing and walk along the old road to the north. This grassy track ends in a mudhole near Quilchena Creek and in the spring the roar of Quilchena Falls, a short distance upstream, can be heard all the way back to the clearing. A trail leads to the base of the falls and a rough path winds up the basalt cliffs to the right of the falls, joining another old road that passes near the crest. You can follow it back down the hill to the original creek crossing near the beaver dam and then retrace your route to the main campground. You can cut four or five kilometres off the round trip hike by parking near the gate at the north end of Alleyne Lake.

Remember that this is private rangeland. Refrain from starting any campfires and carry out whatever you carry in. Through careful attention to detail and respect for the rights of cattlemen, we can continue to enjoy the privilege of access across private land.

Fig. 19: Bears like rose hips.

Wildflowers, wildlife, waterfowl, excellent fishing, one-metre-thick ponderosa pine and equally large Douglas fir are all features of a two-hour pocket wilderness hike around Kentucky Lake. The four kilometre loop trail is well marked and most easily found on the northeast side of Kentucky Lake near the campground. Small red aluminum "flags" nailed to trees act as a guide in some areas, but the trail is virtually impossible to lose. It is an easy hike around the lake—even easier with a mountain bicycle (motorized bikes are prohibited).

The completion of the Okanagan Connector (Hwy 97C) will undoubtedly see increased pressure put on the resources of the Kentucky-Alleyne area. With care, commonsense and government support, fishermen, campers, hikers, ranchers and loons will continue to enjoy the rugged beauty, good fishing, excellent hiking and other recreational benefits of the upland lakes.

●●●

The Okanagan Connector

(Highway 97C)

Statistics	For map, see page 111.
Distance:	90 km, Aspen Grove to Westbank.
	115 km, Merritt to Westbank.
Travel Time:	Approximately one hour.
Condition:	Four-lane, divided highway except for a two-lane section north of Aspen Grove. Limited access.
Topo Maps:	Ashcroft 92 I (1:250,000).
	Hope 92 H (1:250,000).
	Penticton 82 E (1:250,000).
Forest Maps:	Merritt - Princeton.
	Penticton and Area.
Communities:	Merritt, Aspen Grove, Westbank & Peachland.

Deer made the first trails across the plateau country separating the Nicola Valley from Okanagan Lake. They moved steadily, driven by the seasons, their need for forest cover while rearing their young, and the never ending search for food. Native Indians followed the game trails, both to find the animals and to trade with other native groups living in the Similkameen, Nicola and Thompson valleys.

Randy Manuel, curator of the R.N. Atkinson Museum in Penticton, researched native Indian trails and prepared a map depicting the main routes followed by the Indians of the South Okanagan and Similkameen. According to Mr. Manuel, Indian trails generally followed streams, but not the deeper canyons or sharply cut chasms of some creeks. The Peachland cut-off trail started at Squ-ha, the bend in Okanagan Lake at Peachland. The trail went through country drained by a creek known as Spil-Kuk-a-Nilh, which means Eagle Nest. The Peachland cut-off trail followed Deep Creek and then headed southwest, eventually joining the Trout Creek Trail from Summerland. The latter rounded the chain lakes area, Link, Chain and Osprey lakes, about 3,600 feet (1100 metres) above sea level and then wound through back valleys to the high bench land northeast of Princeton.

David Stuart, of the Pacific Fur Company, headed the first white party to travel the trails through the Okanagan Valley. In September, 1811, his party of fur traders, assisted by friendly Indian guides, travelled as far north as Kamloops. They quickly established the plateau trail network as part of their trade route from the Interior to the Pacific Ocean at the mouth of the Columbia River.

In 1859, as the fur trade waned and the Fraser River gold rush flourished, the plateau trails began to feel the traffic of miners. Initially, their destination was the bars of the Fraser, but Tranquille Creek, near Kamloops, and Granite Creek, northwest of Princeton, soon attracted their attention. Then, as interest shifted to the Boundary District, the gold rush traffic moved in the opposite direction. Rock Creek became a destination of choice.

Ranchers, loggers and prospectors turned the horse trails into wagon roads. These, in turn, were slightly improved by crews building high voltage power lines. But, from a recreational perspective, the plateau route from the Nicola Valley to the Okanagan Valley remained the domain of the fishermen, hunter and backroad explorer.

The idea of a highway across the plateau is not a new one. Earlier this century, members of the former Kelowna Board of Trade, now the Kelowna Chamber of Commerce, began to promote this alternate route to Merritt. For many years, the board of trade organized a cavalcade of vehicles to the trek from Kelowna to Merritt during the early summer months. Until the opening of the Okanagan Connector (Highway 97C) on October 1, 1990, determination and a pick-up truck were prerequisites for a successful cross-country trip from Merritt to Kelowna.

According to the B.C. Ministry of Transportation and Highways, the 108 kilometre long route connecting Coquihalla Highway 5 at Merritt with Highway 97, between Peachland and Westbank, was completed one year ahead of schedule and at the budgeted cost of $225 million. The Okanagan Connector also cut one and one half hours off the usual highway travelling time between the Lower Mainland and the Central Okanagan. It also reduced the travel time between Merritt and Kelowna by half.

Fig. 20: Pothole Lake.

From an outdoor recreation perspective, the Okanagan Connector (Highway 97C) has its greatest value as a *connector*. It improves access to the Okanagan's five ski hills for Nicola Valley and Lower Mainland residents. It also means reduced travel time for Okanagan fishermen heading for the lakes surrounding Merritt. However, the highway appears to have been deliberately designed to serve as a throughway, with little access to the many fine lakes of the Douglas and Okanagan plateau region.

The reasons behind this limited access, according to government sources, are several. Uppermost in mind is the inability of the fragile upland lakes to withstand the onslaught of tens of thousands of new visitors. Pennask Lake, the source of a large portion of B.C.'s Rainbow trout hatchery eggs, is too close to the highway for comfort. Over-fishing at Pennask Lake, a source of hatchery stock, would have detrimental effects on fishing throughout the Interior. The numerous small lakes in the Paradise Lake area would also suffer a similar fate.

Ranching interests, particularly the Douglas Lake Cattle Company, are also opposed to wide open access to the plateau region.

Their concerns included loss of valuable rangeland to highway right-of-way and increased cattle harassment.

A detailed description of the route serves little purpose, but here are a few highlights. With the junction of Highway 5A and 97C as the km 0 reference, you will get a clear view of Alleyne Lake as you descend the hill near km 3.2. (See *Kentucky-Alleyne Provincial Park*.) Although not as easily seen when travelling east, Pothole Lake is visible on the north side of the road near km 7.2.

The Loon Lake Road exit at km 16.0 can take you south into a land of lodgepole pine and upland meadows. The gravel backroads also provide an alternate route past Loon Lake to Kentucky-Alleyne Provincial Park and Highway 5A, south of Aspen Grove.

The Elkhart Road exit at km 30 offers little in the way of recreational opportunities at this time, but there is a restaurant/service station 1.8 kilometres off the highway. According to Forest Service sources, access may soon be allowed into the Paradise Lakes area.

Sunset Main Road, near km 42, also provides access to the plateau country. There is a 6.7-kilometre-long rough gravel road along the north slopes of Pennask Mountain that links the interchange with the Bear Forest Service Road which winds northeast down to Okanagan Lake near Bear Creek Provincial Park. Sunset Main Road continues southeast into the Headwaters Lakes area before descending into Peachland. (See *Pennask Lake Road*.)

The Okanagan Connector crests near km 54 (about 1728 metres or 5670 ft above sea level) and begins the 32 kilometre runway to the Okanagan. The highway skirts the Trepanier Creek canyon, passing the Brenda Mine tailing pile near km 63.

B renda Mine, a copper/molybdenum operation, closed in 1990 after two decades of production. A quartz vein on the site was originally worked by the Sandbergs of Kelowna in the late 1930s and early 1940s as the "Copper King" property. It was then abandoned until re-discovered in 1954 by Bob Bechtel, a Penticton prospector. It took ten years of effort before Brenda Mines Ltd. was formed and another five years and $62.5 million before the mine began production in 1970. A member of the Noranda Group, Brenda produced approximately 278,000 tonnes of copper, 66,000 tonnes of molybdenum, 125 tonnes of silver and two tonnes of gold.

There is an ungulate overpass about seven kilometres from the bottom of the hill that is said to be the first of its kind in Canada.

The rest area/information centre a few kilometres from the junction with Highway 97 provides the last stop before reaching the two-lane traffic corridor between Peachland and Westbank.

●●●

Merritt to Kamloops

(Coquihalla Hwy 5)

Statistics   **For map, see page 4.**

Distance:	80 km.
Travel Time:	Less than one hour.
Condition:	Paved, divided highway.
Topo Maps:	Merritt 92 I/SE (1:100,000).
	Kamloops 92 I/NE (1:100,000).
Forest Maps:	Merritt - Princeton.
Communities:	Merritt & Kamloops.

Exit 290, on the northeast side of Merritt, marks the junction to Highway 5A and Nicola Lake. It also signals the start of the long climb out of the Nicola Valley. A pull-out six kilometres north of the interchange provides a view of Nicola Lake and the pioneer settlement of Nicola. This view has changed little in the past century: cattle still graze on the grassland and the Nicola River still twists and turns along the valley floor.

Another 10 kilometres up the hill, the view disappears, blocked out by Mount Mabel as Highway 5 enters the confines of the Clapperton Creek valley. Helmer Road (Exit 315) is usually closed to traffic beyond the interchange loop in the summer months to protect the fragile upland environment. But in winter, the gates are opened to snowmobilers and 1723-metre-high Swakum Mountain becomes a beehive of droning machines.

Using the BC Hydro right-of-way, old roads and some especially cut trails, the Swakum Mountain Trail Riders Association and the Forest Service have created approximately 78 km of interlocking trails on the mountain to the west of the highway. In the past these trails have been maintained and periodically groomed by staff working under the funding of employment grants.

Coquihalla Highway 5 crests at about 1450 metres (4700 ft) in the upland plateau about six kilometres north of the Helmer Road exit. If you look carefully through the trees to the east, you may catch a glimpse of Surrey and Sussex lakes. These fine fishing holes are not accessible from Highway 5, but can be reached from the Logan Lake Road, west of Exit 336. (See *Surrey Lake Road* for details.)

Although these huge animals don't usually stick around to be photographed, moose can often be seen in the marshes of the Meadow Creek Valley, between the crest and the Walloper Lake interchange (Exit 336). The chain link fences along the route in this area were installed to protect highway travellers and big game from each other.

Walloper Lake is just one of the reasons to leave the freeway at Exit 336. Lac Le Jeune Provincial Park and several Forest Service recreation sites also lie to the east of the highway, on or near the old road from Logan Lake to Kamloops. (See *Logan Lake Road* and *Chuwels Mountain Road* for details.) To the west is the access to Surrey Lake as well as the community of Logan Lake and the giant open-pit copper mines of the Highland Valley.

If you are continuing along Highway 5 toward Kamloops, a quick glance to the right (south) will reveal the ski slopes of the Lac Le Jeune Ski Ranch. Also accessible from Exit 336, this resort offers downhill and cross-country skiing plus overnight accommodations, food services and a conference centre.

The brake check pull-out marks the top of the long hill down to Kamloops and the Trans-Canada Highway (Exit 362). A word of caution as you approach the Trans-Canada Highway—the speed limit changes from 110 to 90 kph. As a second caution, watch the signs carefully as you continue northeastward. The Columbia Street interchange (Exit 369) can be confusing. Keep to the inside or centre lane if you want to bypass Kamloops and keep to the right lanes if downtown is your destination.

Exit 374 marks the departure from the freeway and the continuation of Highway 5 (The Yellowhead Route) toward Jasper. The four-lane highway continues eastward as the Trans-Canada Highway (1/97), becoming a two-lane highway east of Kamloops.

●●●

Merritt to Ashcroft

(Highway 97C)

Statistics	For maps, see pages 4 & 100.
Distance:	44 km, Hwy 8 at Shulus to Logan Lake.
	60 km, Logan Lake to Ashcroft.
Travel Time:	2 hours.
Condition:	Paved throughout.
Season:	All seasons.
Topo Maps:	Merritt 92 I/2 (1:50,000).
	Mamit Lake 92 I/7 (1:50,000.
	Spences Bridge 92 I/6 (1:50,000).
	Ashcroft 92 I/11 (1:50,000).
Forest Maps:	Merritt - Princeton.
Communities:	Merritt, Logan Lake & Ashcroft.

The Mamit Lake Road portion of Highway 97C, in addition to being the main link between Merritt and the copper mines of the Highland Valley, was once the route of gold seekers travelling from the Similkameen to the Cariboo.

Mamit Lake Road leads north from Highway 8 at the Indian community of Shulus, five kilometres west of Merritt. It passes through dry bunchgrass and sagebrush country before entering scattered timber as it climbs the Guichon Creek valley. Approximately four kilometres north of the Highway 8 junction, the hillside workings of the Craigmont copper mine can be seen across the valley. Craigmont, which closed in 1983, once employed over 600 men.

Several side roads lead to ranches, lakes and logging operations on the plateau country to the east of Mamit Lake. The Mamit Lake area was the Nicola Valley's French district, first settled in 1873 by Joseph and Pierre Guichon and later by Louis Quenville and Jean and Francois Rey. Joseph Guichon later established a ranch on the southeast shores of Nicola Lake and, in 1907-08, built the famous Quilchena Hotel.

Mamit Lake Road ends at the copper mining community of Logan Lake, where the Highland Valley Road, newly-designated as Highway 97C, continues to Ashcroft and other roads branch off to Savona and Kamloops.

Fig. 21: Cross-country skiing near Logan Lake.

Logan Lake is a community that has seen more than its fair share of ups and downs. Because of the mines, its fate has been tied to the vagaries of world copper prices. Logan Lake District Council has attempted to diversify the community employment base and the village tax rolls. Logan Lake has been successful in encouraging retired people to move into the relatively low-cost housing. It has also been successful in creating a recreational environment that would be the envy of other communities of similar size. (See Logan Lake Road for additional information on outdoor recreation in the area.)

Cross-country skiing has become a major winter pasttime. The cross-country ski trail network starts near a television tower above the village and extends to the north. At the time of writing, the Highland Valley Outdoor Association had 34 kilometres of groomed cross-country trails including two kilometres of lighted track. The system has something for everyone with beginner trails near the community and a mixture of intermediate and advanced trails throughout the network.

Highland Valley Road bisects North America's largest copper mine. With the first claims in the Guichon Batholith staked in 1896, mining and exploration proceeded sporadically for more than a half century before technological developments made mining of the low grade deposit profitable.

H.H. "Spud" Huestis and his associates formed the Bethlehem Copper Corporation in the mid-1950. Bethlehem Copper began an intensive exploration program that established copper/molybdenum ore reserves exceeding 60 million tonnes at approximately five per cent copper. After several attempts at financing, Japan's Sumitomo Metal Company invested $5.5 million, and on 1 December 1962, Bethlehem Copper began production.

Egil Lorntzsen, another British Columbia mine-finder of note, first staked claims in 1958-59 on what became the Lornex Mining Corporation property (now Highland Valley Copper). It took more than a decade before a $144 million construction program led to Lornex's first shipment of copper concentrate in July 1972. In its first decade of operation, Lornex expanded to become a giant open-pit mine employing 1,100 people. It used some of the world's largest mining equipment, including specially designed 235-tonne capacity, rubber-tired haulage trucks.

In 1980-81, Highmont Mines went into production east of the Lornex pit. Plans were also underway for an even larger mine on the valley floor on claims owned by Valley Copper (Cominco). After hundreds of millions of dollars were spent, Valley Copper did come on line, but with a new name and new partners. Cominco, Lornex and Highmont combined to form Highland Valley Copper. The Lornex mill was expanded by moving the Highmont Mill to the

Lornex site. The Valley Copper ore body is now being processed by carrying the ore up to the Lornex mill in giant conveyors.

In 1990, Highland Valley Copper employed 1,220 people to mine 300,000 metric tonnes of ore and waste daily. The 235-tonne trucks were phased out in favor of 170 and 190 tonne capacity haul trucks, supported by huge electric shovels and other heavy equipment.

Fig. 22: Mine haul truck on display at Logan Lake.

Highland Valley Road (97C) links the District of Logan Lake with Ashcroft, on the Trans-Canada Highway. This scenic drive climbs gradually into the giant ancient volcanic crater that is the Highland Valley. Approximately 16 km west of Logan Lake, the road passes the former Lornex and Bethlehem Copper operations (now part of Highland Valley Copper) before skirting the growing cavity created by the Valley Copper pit. The road continues the gradual ascent, avoiding the giant tailing pond that collects the mill waste. Then, after reaching the height-of-land, it begins the steep descent into the semi-desert country surrounding Ashcroft.

In the past, Highland Valley Copper has offered mine tours at 10 a.m. and 1 p.m. on normal working days. If you can't visit the real thing, one of the huge trucks is on display at Logan Lake.

●●●

Logan Lake Road

(Logan Lake to Kamloops)

Statistics	For map. see pages 4 & 100.
Distance:	53 km via Logan Lake / Lac Le Jeune Road.
	24 km to Exit 336 on Coquihalla Highway 5.
Travel Time:	Less than one hour.
Condition:	Paved throughout.
Topo Maps:	Merritt 92 I/SE (1:100,000).
	Kamloops 92 I/NE (1:100,000).
Forest Maps:	Kamloops and Area.
Communities:	Logan Lake, Lac Le Jeune and Kamloops.

With the crossroads to the Logan Lake rec centre as km 0, the highway from Logan Lake to Kamloops skirts the west side of the lake before following the Meadow Creek valley upstream as far as Lac Le Jeune. If fishing is your fancy, you can turn off at km 1.2 for the picnic area and parking lot at the north end of the lake. If you would rather swing at something that doesn't bite or swing back, the Meadow Creek Golf Course is only a few seconds farther along the road.

For some high-country fishing and backroad exploring, head north on Paska Lake Road at km 15.3. Mile High Lodge, on Face Lake, is 11 kilometres north of the highway. It offers cottages and a campground with more amenities than many fishing camps. Dominic Lake Resort is 17 kilometres north of the highway. It offers slightly fewer amenities and is a little higher in altitude although both lakes are close to 1500 metres (5,000 feet) above sea level. You can continue another 56 kilometres north of Dominic Lake and emerge on the Trans-Canada Highway, west of Kamloops.

Surrey Lake Forest Service Road at km 16.3 offers you another option for high altitude fishing, backroad exploring and camping. Surrey Lake is about 10 kilometres south of the Logan Lake Road and just east of the summit of the Merritt-Kamloops section of Coquihalla Highway 5. If you welcome mud holes as a challenge, you can try fishing at Sussex Lake, Bob Lake or the Frogmoore Lakes. Make sure you have a winch, as the big one you may want to pull in could be your vehicle—not a wild and wily Kamloops trout.

The Lac Le Jeune Interchange (Exit 336) is 24 kilometres east of Logan Lake. If you are not in a hurry, take the old route down to Kamloops—you will find plenty of recreational opportunities year around. To make it easier should you be leaving Coquihalla Highway 5 at Exit 336, reset your odometer to zero here and begin the count again.

Walloper Lake Fishing Resort, at km 1.0, offers summer fishing plus ice-fishing, cross-country skiing and skating in the winter. It is next to the highway so you don't have to worry about digging out the tire chains in winter.

Lac Le Jeune Road, at km 3.6, provides access to a resort, ski hill, cross-country ski trail, lake and provincial park, all under the Lac Le Jeune name. Woody Life Village Resort is 0.6 kilometres off the Logan Lake Road, while the provincial park campground, is another half kilometre farther along.

With Exit 336 as reference, the Stake Lake Forest Service Recreation Area Picnic Ground is at km 6.5 and the Chuwels Mountain Road and underpass is at km 6.6. See Chuwels Mountain Road for details on the drive to the 1896 metre peak.

Hidden off the highway at km 8.5 is the McConnell Lake Forest Service Recreation Site. Although it doesn't have any services or supervision, camping is free and the fishing can be good. McConnell Lake also marks the beginning of the long descent to Kamloops.

Edith Lake Road at km 13.0, offers another backroad diversion. If luck and conditions are with you, you could end up at Knutsford on Highway 5A, after a pleasant drive through the back country.

North of Edith Lake Road, Logan Lake Road continues its descent, leaving the timber behind and entering the grasslands as it skirts the east side of Sugarloaf Hill and reaches Coquihalla Highway 5 at the weigh scales at km 27. Unfortunately, you will have to drive parallel to Highway 5 for another two kilometres before gaining access at the Copperhead Drive Interchange (Exit 366)

●●●

Surrey Lake Road

For map, see page 100.

Statistics

Distance:	12.4 km, Logan Lake Road to Sussex Lake.
Travel Time:	Less than one hour.
Condition:	Gravel road, some very rough sections.
Season:	Summer and early fall.
Topo Maps:	Mamit Lake 92 I/7 (1:50,000).
Forest Maps:	Merritt - Princeton.
Communities:	Merritt, Logan Lake & Kamloops.

The face of the plateau country southwest of Kamloops has certainly changed since Walter Humphrey established the Surrey Lake Fishing Camp in 1931. Much of the original dirt road that wound up from Kamloops has disappeared under the black-top of successive incarnations of the Lac Le Jeune / Logan Lake Road and, most recently, the Coquihalla Highway, Phase II.

While the Coquihalla Highway passes within a long stone's throw of Surrey Lake and Sussex Lake, there is no direct access. Instead, access to Surrey Lake is from the Logan Lake Road, 7.5 km west of the Walloper Lake Interchange (Exit 336). The thick stand of lodgepole pine surrounding the lakes muffle the highway noise and the nearness of "civilization" is soon forgotten.

With the Logan Lake Road / Surrey Lake Forest Service Road junction as km 0, the Surrey Lake Road winds south through a mixture of open fields, lodgepole pine and aspen groves. It crosses Meadow Creek near km 1 and passes the west end of Desmond Lake at km 4. Although there is no recreation site or boat launch ramp at Desmond Lake, it is possible to snake a canoe or cartop boat through the reeds and out into the lake.

Fig. 23: Desmond Lake.

Beyond Desmond Lake, the road continues to climb through the pine, passing under the Coquihalla Highway at km 7.4. Keep left at km 7.9, following the main logging road southeast for another half kilometre. The Surrey Lake Resort sign at km 8.3 marks the beginning of the rough 1.5 km-long-road into Surrey Lake.

The privately-owned resort is at the north end of Surrey Lake, but there is public access and a Forest Service recreation site on the west side. The road, extremely rough and full of water-filled potholes in the summer of 1990, continues along the west side of Surrey Lake, passing the dammed outlet at km 11.6. It then winds through the trees to Sussex Lake, ending for all intents and purposes, at km 12.4 and the Sussex Lake Forest Service recreation site. According to the maps, the linear mud hole loosely called a road does continue south to Bob Lake.

If fishing, wilderness camping or backroads exploring interests you, Surrey and Sussex lakes are certainly worth checking. Unlike some of the marshy upland lakes, Sussex Lake does have a sandy bottom that could be conducive to swimming—if there has been a week or two of hot weather to warm the water.

If the logging roads are kept open in winter, the Surrey-Sussex area could also be a destination for cross-country skiing and ice fishing. If you prefer the atmosphere of a resort, write the Surrey Lake Fishing Resort, P.O. Box 489, Kamloops, B.C. V2C 5L2.

●●●

Chuwels Mountain Road

Statistics	For map, see page 100.
Distance:	12 km from Logan Lake Road to the peak.
Travel Time:	Approximately 1/2 hour in dry weather.
Condition:	Gravel road with rough sections.
Season:	Summer and early fall.
Topo Maps:	Kamloops 92 I/NE (1:100,000).
Forest Maps:	Kamloops.
Communities:	Kamloops & Logan Lake.

If you have ever wanted to get to the top, Chuwels Mountain is one place you can do it. This 1896-metre-high timber-clad peak lies north of Lac Le Jeune and south of Kamloops Lake and is easily accessible from the Logan Lake Road. Chuwels Mountain Road starts just north of the Stake Lake recreation site, and after passing under Coquihalla Highway 5, begins its ascent.

The Lodgepole Lake Forest Service rec site near km 4 offers a camping alternative to the provincial park at Lac Le Jeune near the Logan Lake Road. If you are heading to the hills for a day of fishing, you may also want to explore the small lake at km 4.7.

For the next four kilometres, the road winds through logged areas before climbing up through the timber to a fork in the road near km 10.5. The new road to the right climbs up to the east peak of the mountain and a radio repeater site. The older road to the left continues to the west peak at km 12 and more radio repeaters.

The view from a rocky knoll just west of the buildings is excellent. Down below lies Paska and Face lakes while on the middle skyline is Greenstone Mountain. The antenna-festooned mountain in the far west is Mount Savona, another interesting viewpoint that has attracted more than passing interest from local rockhounds.

•••

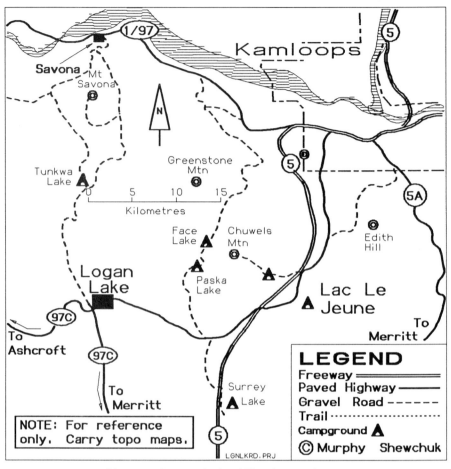

Map 12: Logan Lake / Kamloops Area.

Merritt to Kamloops

(Highway 5A)

Statistics	For map, see page 4.
Distance:	98 km from Merritt to Kamloops via Hwy 5A.
Travel Time:	One to one and one half hours.
Condition:	Paved throughout.
Season:	All season.
Topo Maps:	Merritt 92 I/SE (1:100,000).
	Kamloops 92 I/NE (1:100,000).
Forest Maps:	Merritt - Princeton.
Communities:	Merritt, Quilchena & Kamloops.

The Nicola Valley is SUN country. On the lee side of the Coast and North Cascade mountain ranges, the valley seldom gets more than 25 cm (10 inches) of precipitation a year—and most of this falls in late spring. Sagebrush, bunchgrass, ponderosa pine and prickly pear cactus thrive in the hot, dry summers.

The Nicola Valley is CATTLE country. The wide open natural grassland is ideally suited for ranching. It is home of the 220,000 hectare (550,000 acre) Douglas Lake Ranch, one of the largest cattle ranches in Canada. Nicola Valley cattlemen ship approximately 15,000 head of beef a year.

The Nicola Valley is RAINBOW TROUT country. The last ice age left thousands of depressions in the Thompson Plateau and, despite the dry climate, many of these have filled with cool, clear water. Nicola Lake, the largest body of water in the valley, is home to over two dozen different species of fish.

The Nicola Valley is FUN country. Just to round out the recreational options, the valley has cross-country skiing, hiking, backpacking and some of the finest wind-surfing lakes in the B.C. Interior.

Merritt, with a population of 7,000, is the commercial centre of the Nicola Valley. It has full tourist facilities including hotels, motels and plenty of stores. Claybanks Park, a new campground, was constructed by the city in 1983.

The Nicola Valley Museum-Archives, located at 2202 Jackson Avenue, officially opened May 1, 1983. It houses an attractive display of local artifacts. It also has a growing collection of original local history material.

Local celebrations are frequent, but the biggest party of all takes place on the Labor Day weekend when the summer climaxes in the Nicola Valley Memorial Rodeo and Fall Fair. Street dancing, pancake breakfasts, old time fiddling contests and a fully-sanctioned rodeo are only part of the extended weekend bash.

The traffic lights at the corner of Nicola Avenue and Voght Street mark an important junction. Straight ahead and Highway 8 will take you to Spences Bridge and the Trans-Canada Highway. Turn to the right and you can cross Coquihalla Highway 5 and continue on Highway 5A past a chain of lakes to Kamloops and the Trans-Canada Highway.

Nicola was an influential Indian chief, but his original name was Hwistesmetxquen, too much of a mouthful for the fur traders of the early 1800s. They named him Nicholas and the name stuck to him as well as numerous geographical features and the settlement of Nicola (km 10).

In the late 1860's, pioneers such as John Clapperton and Edwin Dalley established a thriving community at the foot of Nicola Lake. Stores, livery stables, a school and a church were constructed. In 1882, Michael Hagen, editor of the Yale Inland Sentinel, wrote "...we were at Fenson's Mills, and here it was we beheld the most business-looking place after leaving Kamloops. The mill power for both the grist mill and saw mill, where also a planer and shingle arrangement were to be seen, was from a fine stream running from the Nicola River."

The community became known as Nicola Lake and in 1905 the name was shortened to "Nicola". A few years later Merritt was established to serve several coal mines and Nicola began its steady decline.

Monck Provincial Park, set among the pines on the north shore of Nicola Lake, is accessible via Monck Park Road at km 11. (See *Monck Provincial Park* for details.)

Ample fish and early ice breakup made Nicola Lake (km 11.5) especially valuable to the local Indians. Nicola Lake contains 26

Fig. 24: Windsurfing on Nicola Lake.

different varieties of fish including mountain whitefish, spring salmon, kokanee, rainbow trout, Dolly Varden char and freshwater ling cod.

The majestic Quilchena Hotel (km 22.5) first opened its doors in 1908. Built by pioneer rancher Joseph Guichon to serve the carriage trade between Nicola and Kamloops, it was heralded as one of the finest hotels in the British Columbia Interior. Polo was common on the nearby meadowland, along with horse racing and rodeos.

Prohibition closed the bar and the hotel in 1919. Then in 1958, Guy Rose, Old Joe's grandson, reopened the hotel and turned the former polo field into a golf course. Today, the Quilchena Hotel is open from May to October, offering fine food and accommodation in the western tradition.

The Pennask Lake Road leaves Hwy 5A at km 25, a short distance north of the Quilchena Hotel. This backroad, extremely rough in places, winds across the plateau to Okanagan Lake, with side roads into some excellent trout fishing lakes. (See Pennask Lake Road for details.)

The Douglas Lake Road, at km 27.6, offers another scenic alternate route to the north Okanagan and Shuswap area, joining Highway 97 at Westwold. The east end of the road can be slippery in wet weather, but otherwise it is quite passable throughout most of the year. Douglas Lake is the headquarters of the Douglas Lake Cattle Ranch, a half-million acre, multi-million dollar operation formerly owned by the late Charles "Chunky" Woodward. (See Douglas Lake Road for details.)

The original Our Lady of Lourdes Catholic Church at the Douglas Lake Road junction was dedicated in 1893. It was built under the supervision of Father Le Jeune from lumber donated by Joseph Guichon. It was destroyed by fire in a suspected arson incident on Monday, September 3, 1979. After considerable discussion and planning, construction of a new log church was begun in 1982. This beautiful red-stained building was completed and held its first services late in 1983.

Beyond Douglas Lake Road, Highway 5A follows the Nicola Lake shoreline to the head of the lake and the Guichon Ranch. The marshes to the north of the Guichon Ranch headquarters are being rehabilitated by Ducks Unlimited to improve resting and nesting conditions for migratory waterfowl.

Peterhope Road, at km 44.2 near the north end of the marshy basin, marks the junction to several fine trout lakes. A rough gravel road climbs eastward, gaining 400 metres in the seven kilometres to Peter Hope Lake. If you are an avid fisherman or backroad explorer, you may wish to tackle the 34-km-long loop that will take you to the Douglas Lake Road via Peter Hope Lake and Glimpse Lake. (See Glimpse Lake Loop for details.)

The rock outcroppings to the southeast of Stump Lake, accessible via the Planet Mine Road at km 45.2, must have been a beehive of activity in the mid-1930's. Twenty veins were being worked to supply 150 tonnes of ore per day to the Planet Mine roller mill and concentrator. Mining activity in the area has ebbed and flowed since 1882 with the most recent excitement taking place in 1983. Gold, silver, lead, zinc and copper were among the minerals recovered from Mineral Hill.

When the first settlers came to the region, there were white stumps still sticking out of Stump Lake, the result of a natural occurrence raising the lake level and flooding the trees. Today the lake is a mass of colorful sails most weekends from May to mid-September as sailing enthusiasts and windsurfers pit their skills against the breeze that is funneled up the valley.

Shepherd's Rock, a large volcanic boulder in a marshy valley to the west of Highway 5A from the "Empire of Grass" stop-of-interest sign at Napier Lake (km 60.4) has historical significance. It is said to be the location where the notorious McLean brothers and Alex Hare murdered sheepherder James Kelly early in December, 1879. Mel Rothenburger detailed the story in his book We've Killed Johnny Ussher! published by Mitchell Press.

The nearby grasslands have also attracted other writers of fiction and non-fiction. Alan Fry's The Burden of Adrian Knowle, published by Doubleday, is set in this area. It is a very readable fictional account of the life of a young rancher. Alex Bulman's Kamloops Cattlemen, published by Gray's, is a history of the Willow Ranch (km 70) and ranching in the Kamloops region.

After a steep seven-kilometre-climb from Shumway Lake, Highway 5A crosses the plateau and then begins its long descent to Kamloops city centre. In the past few decades, the city has extended southward until it now takes much of the settlement of Knutsford (km 83.5). The land in this area was used for ranching at least as early as the 1850's. The 1904-1914 period saw a spurt of farming activity on the plateau. Two of these farmers; J.S. Jones and Robert Begbie Longbridge, opened a store and Post Office in 1812, naming it after Knutsford, Longbridge's birthplace in Cheshire.

Highway 5A and 5 rejoin at km 92.5, near the Aberdeen Mall shopping centre. The exact origin of the name "Kamloops" appears to be lost, except to say that there is strong suspicion that it was derived from the Native Indian language.

Was it "Cumcloups", "Kam-a-loops" or "Kam-a-loo-la-pa"? Did it mean "meeting of the waters", referring to the junction of the North and South Thompson rivers or did it mean "meeting place of the people" because it was an important trading campsite?

The subtleties of the name have been left to the historians and students of the Thompson and Shuswap Native languages to decide. Meanwhile Kamloopsians go about making it a vibrant community that fits both descriptions. This is the meeting place of rivers, highways, railways, and airlines. Most important of all, people meet here to live, trade and enjoy life.

●●●

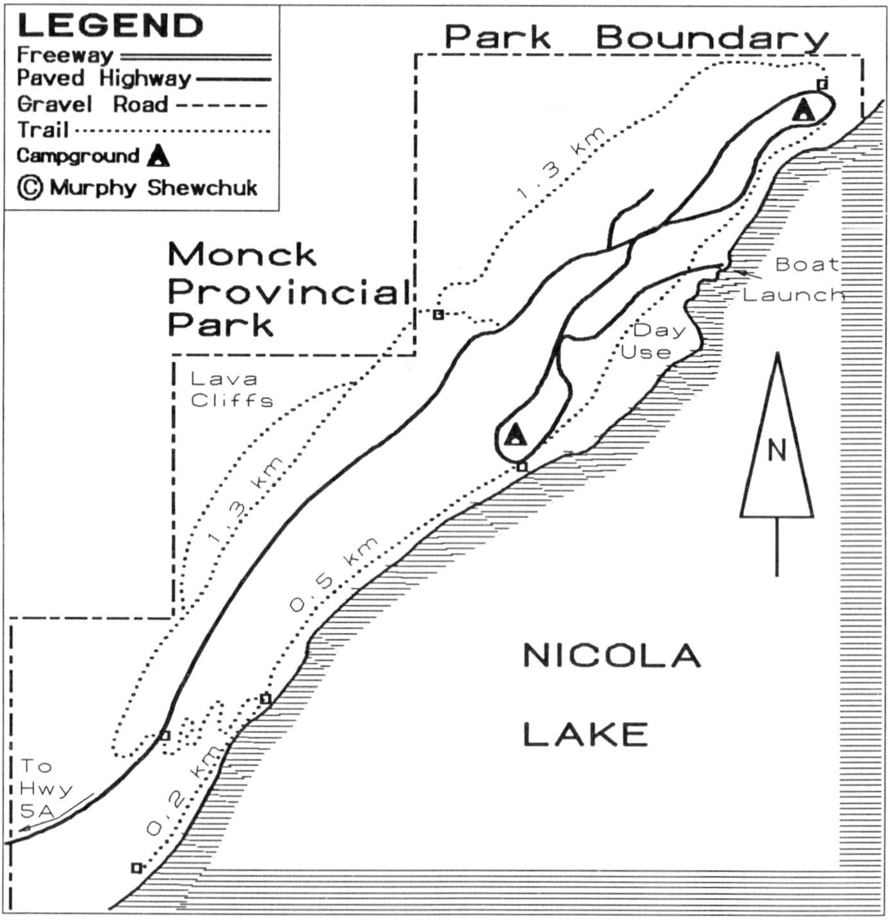

LEGEND
Freeway ═══════
Paved Highway ────
Gravel Road ─ ─ ─ ─
Trail ·············
Campground ▲
© Murphy Shewchuk

Park Boundary

Monck Provincial Park

Lava Cliffs

1.3 km

1.3 km

0.5 km

0.2 km

To Hwy 5A

Boat Launch

Day Use

N

NICOLA

LAKE

Map 13: Monck Provincial Park.

Monck Provincial Park

For map, see page 106.

Statistics	
Distance:	11.2 km, Hwy 5A at Nicola to Monck Park.
Travel Time:	One quarter hour.
Condition:	Paved throughout.
Season:	Accessible year around.
Topo Maps:	Merritt 92 I/SE (1:100,000).
Forest Maps:	Merritt - Princeton.
Communities:	Merritt.

Major Charles Sydney Goldman donated the land that served as the nucleus for Monck Provincial Park in honour of his son, Lieutenant-Commander Penryn "Pen" Monck, a British Navy World War II war hero. Penryn Monck officially changed his name to Monck (an old family name) in 1941, some say to improve his chances of survival should his ship be captured by the German fleet.

C.S. Goldman was born in Bungherdorp, South Africa in 1863. At an early age he was a partner in a large gold and diamond firm at Johannesburg. Goldman later served as a Member of Parliament in England before coming to the Nicola Valley in 1919. Shortly after his arrival, Goldman purchased 6550 acres of land situated between Merritt and Nicola, including much of the townsite of Nicola and a power dam on the Nicola River. Starting with a couple of hundred cattle, Major Goldman built the Nicola Stock Farms Ltd. up to over 5000 head. Major Goldman, who died on April 3, 1958, and his wife Lady Agnes lived in the Nicola Valley for 39 years.

Monck Provincial Park is a 71 unit campground set among the ponderosa pines on the north shore of Nicola Lake. Access is via the 11.2-km-long Monck Park Road which leaves

Highway 5A, 11 km northeast of Merritt. The park is equipped with picnic tables, boat launching ramp, drinking water, a landscaped beach area and change houses.

Fig. 25: Pictographs at Second Beach.

Trails have been developed on the mountainside above the park, leading to an ancient volcanic outcropping. There is also an old road/hiking trail along the lakeshore northeast of the park that leads to Second Beach and a fine example of Indian rock paintings (pictographs). The hike to Second Beach will take at least an hour each way, but the opportunities to photograph wildlife and dry-country wildflowers could make it worth the effort.

Monck Park is also a good summer base for exploring the Nicola Valley. In addition to programs by the Park Naturalist, the park draws on outside resource people to present a varied perspective of the region.

●●●

Pennask Lake Road
(Nicola Lake to Okanagan Lake)

Statistics	**For map, see page 111.**
Distance:	95 km, Quilchena to Peachland.
	120 km, Quilchena to Westside Road.
Travel Time:	Three to four hours in good weather.
Condition:	Gravel, some rough sections.
Season:	June to October.
Topo Maps:	Douglas Lake 92 I/1 (1:50,000).
	Paradise Lake 92 H/16 (1:50,000).
	Peachland 82 E/13 (1:50,000).
Forest Maps:	Merritt - Princeton.
	Penticton and Area.
Communities:	Merritt, Kelowna, Westbank & Peachland.

Pennask Lake, on the Douglas Plateau southeast of Quilchena and west of Kelowna, has a history that is both unusual and colorful. Among the more famous royal personalities to spend time at this upland lake are the American Pineapple King, James Dole, and Queen Elizabeth II and Prince Philip of England.

The first rough road into Pennask Lake wound eastward through the grasslands from Quilchena, via Minnie Lake and through the mud holes in the upland stands of lodgepole pine. It was no easy task to get there, even in the best of weather. And the worst of weather could mean days stuck in the quagmire. In the late 1960s, the opening of the Brenda Mines copper/molybdenum property helped provide easier access to Pennask Lake from Peachland, on Okanagan Lake. Construction of a 138,000 volt power line from Nicola Substation to Brenda Mine and, in 1980-81, a 500,000 volt line from Nicola Substation to the Kootenays opened a 93-km-long dry-weather road from Quilchena to Peachland.

Although considered a public road, it is not currently being maintained by the Ministry of Highways. Instead, various users such as BC Hydro and logging companies maintain it when necessary. Camper trucks and smaller recreational vehicles do make the trip during the dry summer months, but not without more than their fair share of bumps and dust.

Access to the west end of Pennask Lake Road is off Highway 5A, approximately two kilometres north of the Quilchena Hotel (25 km northeast of Merritt). The road climbs steadily for the first 10 km before levelling out on the Douglas Plateau.

After leaving Nicola Lake, the first visible signs of man's activities are a group of corrals and buildings nestled near a small lake in a stand of aspen and cottonwood, 14 km southeast of Highway 5A. The Quilchena Dry Farm was established in 1913 as a provincial government experiment to determine if the natural grasslands surrounding the Nicola Valley were suitable for homesteading. For eight years, the government-employed farmers dealt with an annual rainfall averaging 25 cm; a maximum of three frost-free months; and temperatures ranging from -30° Celsius to +35° Celsius. Then, in 1920, just as a good crop of oats was maturing, a plague of grasshoppers destroyed the entire year's work. The government immediately abandoned the experiment and the land reverted to cattle range.

Minnie Lake, near km 20, was given its name by Byron Earnshaw after his daughter Minnie. Earnshaw and his Indian wife, Shinshinelks, settled in the area in the 1870s. Brian K. de P. Chance, a long-time manager of the Douglas Lake Ranch, first proposed that Minnie Lake be declared a waterfowl sanctuary in 1939. Since the 1941-42 season, many thousands of ducks, geese, swans and pelicans have rested unmolested on their twice-annual fly-past. A locked ranch gate near km 20 restricts access to Minnie Lake and this portion of the Douglas Lake Ranch.

A sign at the junction near km 22 marks a side road that winds 16 kilometres northward and down to Douglas Lake and the Spahomin Indian Reserve. This is the last chance to consider an alternate route across the plateau without having to backtrack.

The road to the right continues eastward to Pennask Lake and Peachland, passing through the Flume Marsh soon after leaving the junction. Several dams on Wasley Creek create or upgrade a total of 75 hectares of marshland as part of Ducks Unlimited Canada's first project on the 220,000 hectare Douglas Lake Ranch. The Flume Marsh, the lowest of the Wasley Creek projects, was so

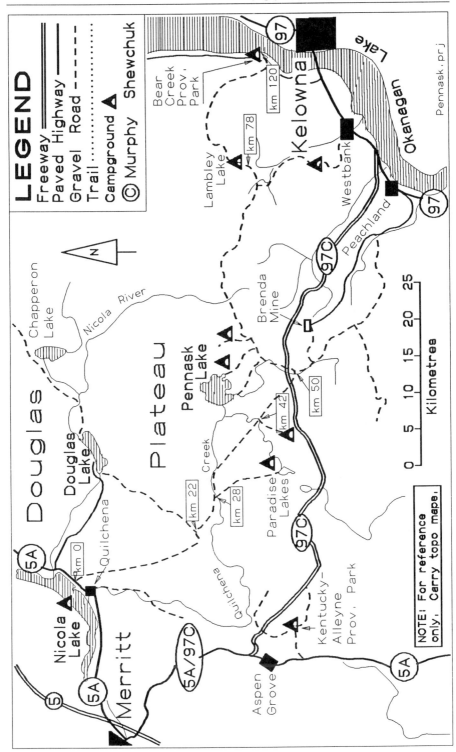

LEGEND

Freeway
Paved Highway
Gravel Road
Trail
Campground ▲
© Murphy Shewchuk

Map 14: Okanagan Connector / Pennask Lake Road.

Fig. 26: Bobs Lake, near Paradise Lake.

named because of the nearby flumes that once carried creek water to the Minnie Lake Ranch hay fields. The dams now control the water to the benefit of waterfowl, moose, deer, muskrat and beaver, and pumps drive the giant irrigation sprinklers.

Paradise Lake Road branches southward off the Pennask Lake Road near the 28 km signpost. There is a resort situated on the northwest corner of Paradise Lake, 13 km to the south, and a Forest Service campsite on nearby Island Lake. Several new roads, built to allow access to the lodgepole pine and a large gravel pit near Bobs Lake, have replaced many of the pothole-ridden roads that formerly linked the nearby lakes. There are nine lakes in the immediate area (elevation 1500 metres) with eight accessible by good trails, creating a fly fisherman's dreamland. Paradise Lakes Resort offers cabins and campsites along with boats for their guests on four of the lakes.

A few minutes drive east of the Paradise Lakes junction the road again forks at km 32. The road to the right dips down across Quilchena Creek and follows the power line right-of-way for about 20 km. The original road to Pennask Lake went straight ahead, but the power line right-of-way is currently the best route although it is extremely rough in spots and impassable in winter and spring thaw.

Another side road near km 42 leads into Reservoir Lake and Skunk Lake. There is a Forest Service recreation site at Reservoir Lake "with very rough four wheel drive access", according to the Forest Service map.

A junction at the east end of the right-of-way road, approximately 50 km from Highway 5A, is of major importance. The construction of the Okanagan Connector (97C) has turned the area into a disaster zone, complete with dead-end roads and detours. After looping under the four-lane highway bridge across Pennask Creek, the gravel road reaches a "T" junction. To the north, the gravel road passes under the highway via a giant culvert before continuing to Pennask Lake and Hatheume Lake and, eventually, to Okanagan Lake near Bear Creek Provincial Park, opposite Kelowna.

If Peachland on Okanagan Lake is your prime destination, the road to the southeast, paralleling the power line, is the right choice. It continues its pothole route past Brenda and MacDonald lakes before joining the pavement near the Brenda Mines office. A second junction a few kilometres before Brenda Lake marks a side road that leads into the Headwaters Lakes area.

The Brenda copper-molybdenum operation was once considered one of the Okanagan Valley's largest mining operations. Work first began on the property in the late 1930s but it was not until the 1970s that the mine went into full production. In the early 1980s, Brenda employed close to 500 men and produced 10,000 tonnes of copper and 2,500 tonnes of molybdenum annually. The mine closed in 1990 when the operation ran out of economical ore.

East of Brenda Mines, the road continues its steady descent into the Okanagan Valley. Much of the remaining 27 km to Okanagan Lake is paved highway—that portion that is not paved is a well-maintained gravel logging road. The route passes the Silver Lake environmental study area, the Peachland cross-country ski area and a second road into the Headwaters Lakes. The road from Brenda Mine reaches Highway 97 on the lake shore at Peachland.

When approaching the Pennask Lake Road from the Okanagan, watch for a traffic light at the junction of Highway 97 and Princeton Avenue on the south side of old Peachland—and take Princeton Avenue up the hill.

James D. Dole, whose name is synonymous with Hawaiian pineapple, first visited Pennask Lake in September, 1927. Accompanied by his wife, Belle, two employees, and three friends who then managed the lodge at Fish Lake (Lac Le Jeune), Dole camped for a week at the head of Pennask Lake.

James Dole was in search of a dream—a dream to be part of a fishing club that could control its surroundings. He wanted a lake of perfect fishing in a region teeming with attractions which he and his friends could call their own. He found it in Pennask Lake and moved quickly to gain control.

In a memorandum dated October 26, 1928, Dole wrote, "We believe that by controlling the land at shore-front we can maintain good fishing in this lake for a long time to come, and it is hoped that it will be kept as a fly fishing lake solely and not be dredged... with tin shops and worms."

The Pennask Lake Club was established in 1929, and officially incorporated in June, 1930, as the Pennask Lake Company, Ltd. Membership was to be limited to fifty at a fee of $1,000.00 per member. Several prominent United States citizens joined the club, but the Great Depression dealt a series of setbacks before Dole's plans could materialize. The new lodge was under-utilized, resulting in deficits that Dole made up from his personal finances. It was not until the late 1940s when the Pennask Lake Fishing and Game Club was formed that new financial life was breathed into the operation—under Canadian control.

The highlight of the club's history is undoubtedly the visit of Queen Elizabeth II and Prince Philip in July, 1959. The Royal visit necessitated months of planning and activity so that the Regal couple could enjoy three days of relaxation in the midst of a hectic Canadian tour.

In 1966-67, Pennask Lake faced its most difficult challenge in the form of an application by Brenda Mines to divert 15,000 acre-feet of water for mining purposes. The Pennask Lake Fishing and Game Club supported local ranchers, the B.C. Wildlife Federation and the provincial Fish and Wildlife Branch in their combined opposition to the Brenda Mines diversion proposal. A two-day public hearing was held in Kamloops in February, 1967. After a delay that lasted until October, 1967, provincial Controller of Water Rights, H.D. De Beck, handed down a decision denying Brenda Mines' applications on Pennask Lake and Pennask Creek.

Dole's dream was saved. Today Pennask Lake continues to be the principal source of Rainbow trout eggs for the provincial restocking program. Fish and Wildlife Branch officials recognize that "Pennask rainbow are genetically superior in terms of fighting ability." In 1970, Pennask Lake was formally established as a "fly fishing only" lake, carrying through with an idea that James Dole, the Pineapple King, had espoused four decades earlier.

The Pennask Lake Fishing and Game Club, with some 165 members, still controls approximately 1,000 hectares of Pennask lake shore and islands. The concept of a private club controlling a prime fishing lake may seem repugnant to some, but trout fishermen all over British Columbia can thank James Dole for the foresight that helped preserve this important fishery resource.

The junction to Pennask Lake Lodge (No Public Access) is approximately six kilometres north of the Okanagan Connector (Hwy 97C) underpass, while the junction to the recreation area is about half a kilometre farther along. Public access is permitted at Pennask Lake Provincial Park on the southeast corner of the lake about six kilometres off the main forest access road.

Pennask Lake Park was first established as a Class A park on May 2, 1974, but it was downgraded to a recreational area early in 1975, and then recently upgraded back to park status. There were several reasons for the interim change. The recreational area status allowed ranching interests to keep their cattle in the area; limited resource development was allowed; but probably most important of all, it limited park development and consequent pressures on Pennask Lake as the province's most important source of rainbow trout eggs. The construction of the Okanagan Connector has prompted some major soul searching on the part of the Parks Branch. At the time of writing, there was no reasonable access to the Pennask Lake Road from Highway 97C. The present rough access road limits the number of visitors to the park, but with a major highway only a short distance away, public pressure will certainly be applied to improve access and facilities at the lake.

About 4.5 km north of the junction to Pennask Lake Park, another side road leads 4.3 km northwest to Pinnacle Lake and Hatheume Lake. Although Hatheume Lake is considerably smaller than Pennask, it also has a widespread reputation as a source of fighting rainbow trout. At the time of writing, Hatheume was a catch-and-release fishery with a further restriction of barbless hooks. There is a small Forest Service recreation site on the south side of Hatheume Lake and a resort, complete with log cabin cottages on the north shore.

Hatheume Lake is also a place to consider options. It is roughly 60 km to Highway 97 at Peachland via Brenda Mine. It is also roughly 65 km to the Westside Road near Bear Creek Provincial Park and another 7 km to Highway 97 overlooking Okanagan Lake near Kelowna.

The Brenda Mine option was covered a few paragraphs back and now space allows us only a few more paragraphs for the Bear Creek option. The forest access road scribes a wide arc as it descends from the plateau to Okanagan Lake. First, as Barton Hills Forest Road, it continues on a generally easterly direction, passing Windy Lake with a small Forest Service rec site before joining a better road near Cameo Lake. The Cameo Lake rec site is one of the busier in the region. From Cameo Lake, the road continues eastward, crossing the height of land between Lacoma Creek and Powers Creek and again into the Lambley Creek drainage.

The road across the upper elevations (1300 to 1500 metres above sea level) is sometimes rough and slow-going. But beyond Lambley (Bear) Lake, the "Bear Lake Main" road is well maintained on the 25 km descent to the pavement at Westside Road.

Caution is required on all the forest roads in the area, as well as logging trucks and equipment are to be expected at any time. Defensive driving is the only survival technique when confronted with a load of logs.

●●●

Douglas Lake Road

(Nicola Lake to Westwold)

Statistics   **For map, see page 119.**

Distance:	80 km from Nicola Lake to Westwold.
Travel Time:	One to 1.5 hours.
Condition:	Mostly gravel with paved sections.
Season:	All season.
Topo Maps:	Merritt 92 I/SE (1:100,000).
	Vernon 82 L/SW (1:100,000).
Forest Maps:	Merritt - Princeton.
Communities:	Merritt, Quilchena, Douglas Lake & Westwold.

In the upper reaches of British Columbia's Nicola Valley lies an empire of bunchgrass, sagebrush, timber and lakes half the size of the province of Prince Edward Island. Bisecting this rich cattle country is a meandering 80-km-long backroad that passes through biotic zones ranging from semi-desert grasslands to cedar forest.

The Douglas Lake Road, gravel for most of its length, leaves Highway 5A at the Quilchena Indian Reserve, 28 km north of Merritt and 68 km south of Kamloops. At the west end of the route from Nicola Lake to Westwold, the narrow road snakes along the lower slopes of a broad valley. Green irrigated hay fields cover the alluvial fan near the river mouth while prickly pear cactus, sagebrush and bunchgrass dot the arid slopes. A twisting line of cottonwoods mark the meandering path of the Nicola River.

Across the valley, a barely visible horizontal line, best seen at sunrise or when the first winter snows dust the rangeland, defines the shoreline of an ancient glacial lake. During the last period of glaciation, which ended some 10,000 years ago, this region was ripped open and reformed by the slowly flowing mass of destruction. As the ice retreated, it created three different glacial lakes.

The first major lake to form in the Nicola Basin was Glacial Lake Quilchena. It reached an elevation of approximately 1000 metres and drained southward into Otter Creek near Aspen Grove. The second, Glacial Lake Hamilton, was formed when the ice plug retreated in the Salmon River Valley permitting eastward drainage through the Douglas Plateau. Some of the shore features of Lake Hamilton are still visible in the form of terraces on the north slope of Hamilton Mountain, southeast of Nicola Lake.

The last of the giant glacial lakes was Lake Merritt. It was formed when the ice melted out of the Campbell Creek Valley and allowed the meltwater to flow northward into the Thompson Valley near Kamloops. As the last ice plug melted out of the lower reaches of the Nicola Valley, it opened the present drainage route and left the shoreline of Glacial Lake Merritt that is now visible from the Douglas Lake Road.

Near the Lauder Road junction (km 7.2), more than a kilometre of steel link fence encloses Nicola Substation, one of B.C. Hydro's largest substations. The maze of steel towers, ceramic insulators and giant transformers serve as a distribution centre for the province.

An ancient weather-beaten cabin sits on the north bank of the Nicola River, approximately three kilometres up Lauder Road. This is known as the Beak Cabin, and according to Nina Woolliams in her book, Cattle Ranch, Charles Miles Beak had a varied and colorful career as a cook, gold miner, cattle drover, butcher and rancher before settling in the Nicola Valley in 1878. In 1883, Beak began a concerted land and cattle purchasing program that quickly made him one of the largest ranchers in the Interior. Later that same year, he formed a partnership with J.B. Greaves that was to establish the base for the giant Douglas Lake Ranch.

Lauder Ranch, a short distance further up Lauder Road, has the distinction of being one of the oldest in the Nicola Valley that is still owned by the founding family. Joseph Dixon Lauder established the ranch in 1876 and it is still operated by his great-grandson John. (See the Glimpse Lake Loop section for more information on Lauder Road and Glimpse Lake, 13.5 km to the north.)

Hamilton Mountain Road is marked by a barbed-wire gate and a Forest Service sign on the crest of the hill overlooking Douglas Lake, near km 12.5. The 5.6 kilometre drive (or hike) affords an excellent view of Douglas Lake and the surrounding plateau grasslands from a natural viewpoint about 2.9 km from the Douglas Lake Road. The broad panorama of the open rangeland is even more easily seen from the Forest Service fire lookout at the 1500 metre peak. (See Hamilton Mountain Road for details.)

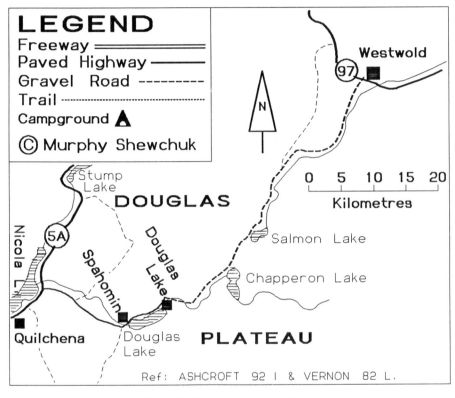

Map 15: Douglas Lake Road.

The Douglas Lake Road crosses the Nicola River at the outflow of Douglas Lake, in the Indian community of Spahomin. The community derives its name from the willows that grow along the shore of Douglas Lake. The young branches of the willows were shaved by the Okanagan Indians and used in the construction of dip nets. The name apparently refers to the many piles of shavings that resulted. Another historic landmark at Spahomin is the Catholic Church that sits well off the road. A side road leads south from Spahomin, into the heart of the Douglas Plateau, joining the Pennask Lake Road near Minnie Lake. Though a little rough, it is usually passable by car in dry weather and can be followed back to Highway 5A near the historic Quilchena Hotel.

At the east end Douglas Lake (km 25) lies the community of Douglas Lake, the main headquarters of the huge Douglas Lake Cattle Company. Formerly owned by the late Charles "Chunky" Woodward of Woodward's Stores fame, this 222,750 hectare (550,000 acre) ranch is considered the largest in Canada.

John Douglas, a Scottish born pioneer of no relation to British Columbia's first Governor, Sir James Douglas, first settled the bottomland near the east end of the lake in 1872. His holdings became part of the nucleus of this vast operation when Charles Miles Beak and "Old Danger" Greaves recognized the potential market of feeding the construction crews of the Canadian Pacific Railway. With the help of a handful of Victoria businessmen, Greaves formed the Douglas Lake Cattle Company. From a foundation built on the lucrative railway contracts, the ranch grew until today it is a multi-million dollar operation. With a staff of close to 50 people, the ranch ships approximately 7,000 white-faced Herefords annually and winters at least 10,000 cattle on hay and grain harvested from their own fields.

East of the ranch headquarters, on the crest of the hill overlooking Sanctuary Lake, is the ranch's private airstrip, capable of handling small jet traffic. The rail-fenced corrals at English Bridge, a short drive further east, is the home of the Panorama cattle sales held each September. Buyers from as far away as Ontario rub shoulders with local politicians, bankers and cattlemen at a beef-and-beer lunch before the auctioneers begin their lively routine. Once the sale gets underway, it usually takes less than an hour for up to 3,500 head of Douglas Lake's prime yearling steers to change hands.

Beyond this last bridge over the Nicola River, the gravel road continues eastward through the open rangeland past Chapperon and Salmon lakes. The group of buildings on the east shore of Chapperon Lake form the headquarters for the eastern operation of the Douglas Lake Ranch. In the early spring, the fields and barns become home to hundreds of new calves while the lakes and marshes provide a resting place for ducks, geese and sandhill cranes on their annual spring migration northward.

Chapperon Lake is also one of the first plateau lakes to open each spring. For this reason, the Okanagan Indians valued the lake and established a fishing camp here in the days long before the influence of the white settlers.

Salmon Lake, 48 km from Nicola Lake on the Douglas Lake Road, is one of several lakes in the Nicola Valley that are restricted to angling with artificial flies. Salmon Lake, like many of the lakes and streams in the region, also has a restricted angling season.

Fig. 27: Cowboy and dog near Douglas Lake Road.

Salmon River drains eastward, eventually emptying into Shuswap Lake at the city of Salmon Arm. For nearly 10 km, it winds through the plateau ranchland, then it descends into a narrow canyon. The Douglas Lake Road follows this same route, leaving the dry grasslands behind and entering the Interior wet belt near km 51. Bunchgrass and ponderosa pine give way to lodgepole

121

pine, Douglas fir and cedar. There is a Forest Service rec site at Weyman Creek (km 61), complete with a mountain trail to a beautiful waterfall. A second site in a meadow alongside the Salmon River at km 66 was once the site of a Dominion Ranger Station. This last site may be difficult to spot when approaching from the west, so watch for a narrow road dipping down into a meadow and you may see the sign.

The bluffs along the roadway near km 70, 10 to 11 km west of Westwold are a favorite haunt of local rock hounds in search of moss and banded agate nodules that can be found in the volcanic rock.

Westwold was originally named Grande Prairie by the nineteenth century fur traders and the Westwold area was often used as a camp for the fur brigades on their way from Kamloops to the Columbia River, via the Okanagan. Westwold also has the dubious distinction of being the final home of the last surviving camel imported to pack supplies during the Cariboo Gold Rush of the 1860s. The camel story began in 1862 when John C. Calbraith of Seton Portage, near Lillooet, purchased 23 bactrian camels at $300 each. Calbraith saw the twinkle of gold when he read that the camels could carry 275 kilograms (600 pounds) of freight and live off the grass and shrubs along the Cariboo road. As with most get-rich-quick schemes, this one had a flaw. The camel's terrible smell frightened livestock and their voracious appetite included everything from sagebrush to miner's socks. In addition to their social unacceptability, their feet could not stand up to the sharp rock on the mountain trails, and the camels were soon turned loose to fend for themselves.

The last of the camels survived until about 1905, spending his last years as a ranch pet in the Westwold area. Finally, when his Oriental premonition warned him that his time had come, it is said that he leaned against the nearest tree and died on his feet.

Today, Westwold and the surrounding Salmon Valley is part of the Shuswap-North Okanagan dairy country, taking advantage of the rich soil and mild climate recognized long ago by the fur traders.

There is always talk of upgrading the Douglas Lake road, usually heard loudest around provincial election time, and surveyors occasional appear—and disappear—with little left to show of their passing except the colorful ribbons. Talk and rumors, however, have been heard in this cattle country for more than a century with little obvious change in the ranching way of life.

●●●

122

Glimpse Lake Loop

For map, see page 126.

Statistics	
Distance:	34 km from Douglas Lake Rd to Hwy 5A.
Travel Time:	One to two hours in dry weather.
Condition:	Gravel road with rough sections.
Season:	Summer and early fall.
Topo Maps:	Merritt 92 I/SE (1:100,000).
Forest Maps:	Merritt - Princeton.
Communities:	Merritt, Quilchena & Kamloops.

This backroads drive from the Douglas Lake Road near B.C. Hydro's Nicola Substation to Highway 5A near Stump Lake offers upland trout fishing, excellent panorama views and a glimpse at the Nicola Valley's colorful past.

The gravel road begins as Lauder Road, 7.2 kilometres east of Nicola Lake on the Douglas Lake Road. It initially skirts the Nicola Substation and then winds down to the Nicola River at km 2.0. The cottonwood trees near the river provide welcome shade on a hot day—and the back-eddies in the stream harbour some fine pan-size trout.

An ancient weather-beaten cabin sits on the north bank of the Nicola River at km 2.6. The Douglas Lake Cattle Company has placed a sign nearby identifying it as the Beak Cabin. According to Nina Woolliams in her book, Cattle Ranch, Charles Miles Beak had a varied and colorful career as a cook, gold miner, cattle drover, butcher and rancher before settling in the Nicola Valley in 1878. In 1883, Beak began a concerted land and cattle purchasing program that quickly made his one of the largest ranches in the B.C. Interior. Later that same year, he formed a partnership with J.B. Greaves that was to establish the land base for the giant Douglas Lake Ranch.

John Lauder's *"Spring Bank Ranch"* (JL), located at km 4.8, has the distinction of being one of the oldest in the Nicola Valley still owned by the founding family. Joseph Dixon Lauder established the ranch in 1876 and it is still operated by his great-grandson John.

A handsome log cabin set near the edge of Lauder Creek at km 6.8 has been the site of several movies in the past decade. Known as the "Abbott Place", the home and ranch was purchased from Hamilton Abbott in the mid-1950s by Joe Lauder. The house served as an office for the CBC production, *Red Serge*, a light comedy series based on the Northwest Mounted Police filmed nearby in 1985 and 1986. The building was also part of the set for the film *"One Boy, One Wolf, One Summer"* undertaken by Gem Productions in 1988.

After passing the Lauder Ranch and the Abbott Place, the road continues to climb steadily through the grasslands, winding in and out of the old creek beds. A long-abandoned cabin and corral at km 9.0 mark the past while cattle on the range and a beaver swimming in a nearby slough are the only signs of present life.

One of the many problems faced by Nicola Valley ranchers is soil erosion triggered by man and beast. A hillside near the cattleguard at km 11 shows the signs of motorbike activity. Some of the ruts in the dust have been carved much deeper by the spring snow melt and frequent summer thundershowers that can dump a considerable amount of rain in a matter of minutes.

The road leaves the grasslands at km 12.5 and enters the timber just before reaching the south end of Glimpse Lake at km 13.5. There is a small Forest Service Recreation Site near the south shore of the lake as well as a boat launch area on the lake. There are private homes along the lake shore and in the trees as well as a second small Forest Service rec site on the north shore of Glimpse Lake.

A junction at km 14.2 marks the first major option since leaving the Douglas Lake Road. The road straight ahead passes a few more homes and a Forest Service recreation site before ending at the Beaver Creek Ranch. The road to the left (west) continues through the subdivision. What has been a good, well-maintained gravel road to this point now becomes somewhat narrower and certainly lumpier as it continues to climb northwest into the timber.

Keep left at the junctions at km 16.6 and km 17.2. The rough cross-road ends on a much better logging road at km 17.4. The road to the east follows the BC Hydro right-of-way toward Westwold and Falkland and may not be passable. Peter Hope Lake lies to the west and this route is usually in much better condition. The route peaks near km 18 at an elevation of approximately 1300 metres (4,265

Fig. 28: Canada Geese.

feet) having climbed about 525 metres since leaving the Douglas Lake Road. It now begins a steady descent, passing under high voltage hydro-electric lines at km 22.2 and 23.5.

The "10K" sign (black lettering on white with a red border) at km 23.7 marks the southeast end of Peter Hope Lake and the distance from Highway 5A near Stump Lake. There is an opening in the trees near this end of the lake that could be a good place to park while fishing among the reeds. There are also several homes along the east shore of the lake. A junction near the "8K" signpost (km 25.8) marks the beginning of a very rough loop road into Plateau Lake. (See "Plateau Lake Loop" for details.)

Continue north along Peter Hope Lake to the large, open Forest Service Recreation Site. Its open layout makes this one of the better recreation sites in the region. Beyond the outlet of the lake, the road begins a steady descent to Highway 5A, passing the entrance road to the Peter Hope Resort near km 27.5. The 400 metre descent in seven kilometres is made a little more difficult by the washboard nature of the gravel road. (Or did the steep grade contribute to the washboard?) Use caution on the turns and narrow sections. Watch for the Peter Hope Resort or "Peterhope Rd" signs when approaching this 34-kilometre-long backroads loop from Highway 5A.

●●●

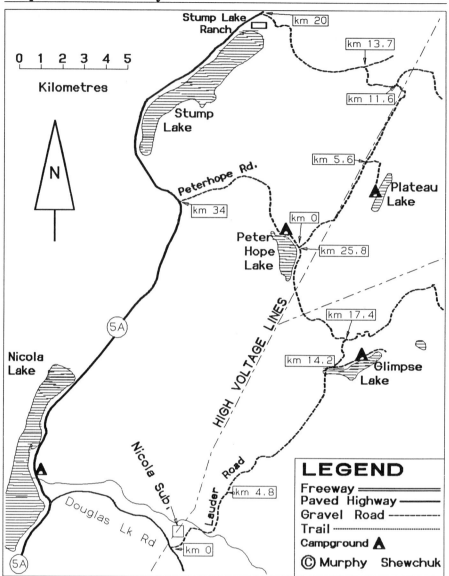

Map 16: Glimpse Lake - Plateau Lake Area.

Plateau Lake Loop

Statistics   For map, see page 126.

Distance:	20 km from Peter Hope Lake to Hwy 5A.
	28 km from Hwy 5A (Peterhope Rd) to Hwy 5A at Stump Lake Ranch.
Travel Time:	One to two hours in dry weather.
Condition:	Gravel road with very rough sections.
Season:	Summer and early fall.
Topo Maps:	Merritt 92 I/SE (1:100,000).
Forest Maps:	Merritt - Princeton.
Communities:	Merritt, Quilchena & Kamloops.

This backroads jaunt into the high country northeast of Merritt has very few redeeming features except for isolation, lots of mud holes and a fine upland lake. If you are out to take your kids for a Sunday drive in the old Chevy, there are safer places to explore. But if the "old Chevy" happens to be a 4x4 pickup with lug tires and lots of clearance and the kids happen to be particularly adept with a chain saw, shovel, winch and fly rod this could be your choice of destination.

The south end of this backroad leaves Peterhope Rd at the 8K sign on the north shore of Peter Hope Lake. Peterhope Rd joins Highway 5A just south of Stump Lake on the old Kamloops-Merritt Highway. (See Glimpse Lake Loop for additional details.)

With the 8K signpost at Peter Hope Lake as the km 0 reference, the rough gravel road runs north, paralleling the high voltage lines although still in the timber.

At km 3.2, the road emerges from the timber and crosses under the 500 kilovolt lines. At this point the road changes from rough to terrible. For the next 2.4 kilometres it skirts mud holes, climbs washed-out slopes and generally tries to make things difficult for man and beast. It was not, however, impassable at the time of writing. A man driving a motorhome and pulling a cartop boat on a trailer also made it through, cursing all the way.

A junction in the middle of the BC Hydro right-of-way at km 5.6 marks the spur road to Plateau Lake. To the right the narrow one-lane cow path winds two kilometres through mud holes and over loose gravel to a beautiful little Forest Service recreation site on the shores of Plateau Lake. Officially posted as a six-unit site, the rec site has provisions for day-use visitors as well as a cut through the reeds that can serve to launch your canoe or cartop boat.

Meanwhile, back at the km 5.6 junction.

If you don't want to face the grueling road from Peter Hope Lake again, you can head north along the right-of-way for about five kilometres to km 11. This section has fewer rocky hills but more potential mud holes, so the choice depends on the season. In spring and early summer, it may be safer to head back to Peter Hope Lake because of the mud holes.

A ssuming you have made it to km 11, follow the road west across the right-of-way and into the lodgepole pine. There are major incremental improvements in the road as it is joined by forest roads coming in from the right at km 11.6 and 13.7. Keep straight ahead at both junctions and you should leave the timber and enter the grasslands high above the Stump Lake Ranch at km 16.3.

Keep to main road as it descends through the grasslands. If you want to stop to enjoy the view of Stump Lake and the ranching scenes below you, pull well off the road in order to avoid conflict with ranch equipment or logging trucks.

The Plateau Lake Loop ends (km 20) at Highway 5A near the Stump Lake Ranch gate just north of Stump Lake and approximately 57 kilometres north of Merritt. The complete backroad loop is about 28 kilometres from Highway 5A back to Highway 5A and will take about two hours under ideal conditions. A serviceable, well-equipped vehicle is a must if you are to avoid a long walk out.

●●●

Hamilton Mountain Road

Statistics	For map, see page 130.
Distance:	5.6 km from Douglas Lake Road to Hamilton Mtn Forest Service Lookout.
Travel Time:	Less than 1/2 hour.
Elevation Gain:	600 metres.
Condition:	Gravel road with rough sections.
Season:	April through October.
Topo Maps:	Merritt 92 I/SE (1:100,000).
	Douglas Lake 92I/1 (1:50,000).
Forest Maps:	Merritt - Princeton.
Communities:	Merritt, Quilchena & Kamloops.

If you are looking for an excellent view of the grasslands of the Douglas Lake Ranch and an opportunity to photograph fairy slippers or chocolate lilies, consider the road to the top of Hamilton Mountain.

Hamilton Mountain Road leaves Douglas Lake Road at the crest of a hill 13 km east of Highway 5A and Nicola Lake. The road climbs up through the grasslands for 1.4 kilometres before entering the light timber that cloaks the dry slopes of the mountain. Cattle and horses often range on these slopes, providing a foreground for a "wild-west" panorama of rolling grasslands and distant mountains.

Fig. 29: Fairy Slipper. (Calypso bulbosa.)

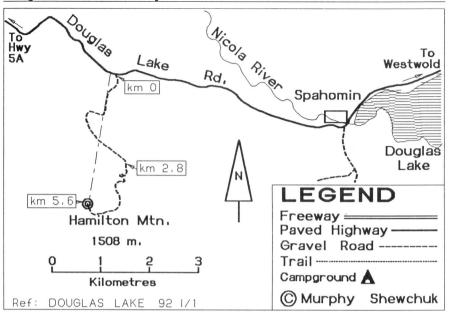

Map 17: Hamilton Mountain Road.

There is a gate at km 2.2 that marks the boundary of the Hamilton Commonage. Just beyond the gate, at km 2.5, a sheltered rock bluff to the right of the road is an ideal spot to photograph calypso orchids and chocolate lilies in May and early June.

The trees are slowly growing up to block what was an excellent view of Douglas Lake at km 2.8. If you scramble a few metres down the slope, you should still be able to capture an impressive image on film, particularly if you get there early enough to see the valley bathed in the morning light.

The narrow dirt road continues to wind around the 1500 metre high mountain, reaching the Forest Service Lookout and a micro-wave radio site at km 5.6. The broad panorama visible from the catwalk of the fire lookout can be particularly interesting. Study the slopes near Douglas Lake and you will see the shorelines of the giant glacial lakes that inundated the valley one hundred centuries ago.

Although rough in a few places, the Hamilton Mountain Road is usually passable with two-wheel drive cars or light trucks in dry weather. However, I would certainly not recommend it for motorhomes or vehicles pulling trailers.

●●●

Chataway Lakes Loop

Statistics	For map, see page 134.
Distance:	32 km Lower Nicola to Chataway Lake.
	29 km Chataway L. to Shackan (Hwy 8).
Travel time:	Half day.
Elevation gain:	Approximately 700 metres (2300 feet).
Conditions:	Partly paved, rough gravel sections.
Season:	Best in dry weather. Closed in winter.
Topo maps:	Lytton, B.C. 92 I/SW (1:100,000).
	Merritt, B.C. 92 I/SE (1:100,000).
Communities:	Merritt, Lower Nicola & Spences Bridge.

The Chataway Lake area, despite the efforts of Bill Roddy and others, has remained relatively unknown to all except the serious angler. The dozen lakes that make up the Chataway group are not famous for particularly large fish, nor are they particularly large themselves. The greatest attraction is the solitude in which a fisherman can cast a fly or drag a lure through the water. Despite the fact that Coquihalla Highway 5 passes through Merritt, 40 road kilometres (25 miles) away, it is still possible to have a lake to yourself, even on a summer Saturday afternoon. And it's still possible to reel in wild rainbow trout when lower elevation lakes are slow.

One of the reasons for Chataway's isolation was the road. Actually, "wagon trail" was probably a better description until Aspen Planers Ltd. of Merritt began harvesting some of the pencil-thin lodgepole pine that grow out of the rocky highlands like quills on a porcupine. The logging efforts required a better route than was available, so a new forest road was carved into the area from the Merritt (Lower Nicola) side. Much of the old road was used, but the new route bypassed some of the muddier and steeper sections, making it possible to take a car or pickup camper into Chataway Lake with little difficulty.

Fig. 30: Craigmont Mine buildings in 1983.

The Chataway Lake adventure starts at Lower Nicola, about 8.5 km west of Merritt on Highway 8. Kilometre 0 is the junction of Aberdeen Road and Highway 8. Follow Aberdeen Road north for 3.3 km and the relentless climb to the highlands begins.

The road twists up a short grade and then the dam and tailing pond of the now closed Craigmont copper mine appears to the left. The Craigmont operation originally began in 1960 as an open-pit mine. At that time it was the first major British Columbia copper mine to open in more than half a century. It had numerous other firsts as well. It was the first to rely on bank loans for much of its $18 million start-up capital which, incidentally, was paid back within three years. And when the open pit had gone as deep as it could safely go, it was one of the first Canadian mines to use the sublevel caving method of underground mining, in which the roof of the mine tunnel is deliberately brought down as the ore is removed.

By the time Craigmont closed in 1983, the mine had produced over 426 million kilograms (947 million pounds) of copper, worth over $450 million. All that remains is a few of the mine buildings and a pile of magnetite powder, a Craigmont by-product that is used in a coal-cleaning slurry in some of BC and Alberta's larger coal mines.

"Chataway" signs mark the junction at km 6.5, a few hundred metres from the mine gate. The gravel road to the right climbs up a draw, passes the local shooting range, and then continues to climb through the ponderosa pine and scrub fir. Be wary of stationary cattle and moving logging trucks.

Stumbles Road, at km 11, (4K on the markers) is the next major intersection. H. Stumbles was a mining man who worked the Eric claim on Promontory Mountain in the 1930s. Although his diamond-drilling efforts missed what was to become known as the Craigmont ore body, he did uncover copper and iron minerals in the form of chalcopyrite and magnetite. Stumbles Road to the right (west) provides access to the north side of Promontory Mountain while the main road continues north to km 14.4 where it again forks. A Chataway sign marked the road to the left as the best route to the plateau country.

If you are interested in mines or prospecting, you may want to detour six kilometers up the old road in search of the remnants of the Aberdeen Mine. Mineral showings were first reported at the Aberdeen Mine site on Broom Creek as early as 1897. Copper was mined at infrequent intervals over the next three decades until 1928 when a major mining effort resulted in gold, silver and over 390,000 pounds (177,000 kg) of copper. Efforts were made in the 1960s to reopen the property, but again excessive water forced its closure.

Meanwhile, back at the junction at km 14.4, a left turn begins a climb northwest on the new road. Known as the Skuhun-Pimainus project on Forest Service maps, construction on this route began in 1985 and continues as budget priorities allow.

In September, 1990, the road was in good condition for most of the way to Pimainus Lake.

The Coquihalla Highway, this is not. With a realistic speed of 50 to 60 kph, everyone but the driver can enjoy the upland plateau scenery. Tyner Lake, everybody's secret fishing hole, lies in a hollow to the west of the road between km 20 and km 23. If you are lucky enough to find the correct backroad into the Tyner Lake Forest Service Recreation Site, it can become your secret fishing hole as well. (Clue: Look for a "No. 4 Rd" marker.)

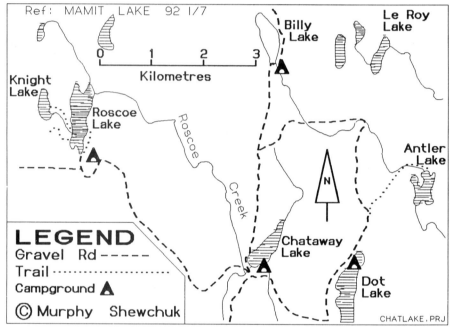

Map 18: Chataway Lakes Area.

The climbing eases considerably around km 20, and the road winds through stands of lodgepole pine and around upland swamps and ponds. Keep right at the Tyner-Skuhun junction at km 22.5. Most of the junctions are marked with "Chataway" signs, some of which are painted on broken paddles or pieces of plank. The last major junction takes you on to the Skuhun Creek Road, one of the original routes to the Chataway area. For the next six kilometres, the road twists and turns up Chataway Creek. The last major junction is at km 32.8, a few hundred metres before the Chataway Lakes Lodge gates. The road to the right is a continuation of the road we left at km 14.4. To right (south east) is Dot Lake and Gypsum Lake plus trails to Antler Lake and Gypsum Mountain. (See Chataway Trails for details.)

Bill Roddy's Chataway Lakes resort offers clean log cabins, a campground and boat rentals. Aside from a recreation room and a few basic supplies, the rest is up to you. Bring your own food, bedding and anything else you might want, including enough fuel to get you back out again. Chataway Lake, at 1310 metres (4300 feet) elevation, stays relatively cool all year around. According to Fisheries Biologist John Cartwright, Chataway and the other lakes in the immediate area are self-sustaining with enough moving water to support proper spawning.

Roscoe Lake, six kilometres northwest of Chataway Lake over a narrow, rough road, is even higher. At 1585 metres (5200 feet), it is on top of the plateau. There is a small Forest Service rec site at the lake and a good hiking trail along its east side. Frequent side roads and survey lines bisect the plateau in this region, primarily as a result of mining exploration. The highlands here form the southern ridge of the Guichon Batholith, a giant crater-like porphyry copper deposit that is now home to Highland Valley Copper, one of the world's largest copper mining operations. A trail from approximately one third the way up the west shore of Roscoe Lake leads into Echo (Knight) Lake. It's only a 10 minute walk, and the rainbow trout fishing can be well worth the effort, even when the rest of the lakes in the area are slow.

Before the recent development of the Skuhun-Pimainus forest road, the Skuhun Creek Road from the west was the better way into the area. Resetting our 0 kilometre reference at the Chataway resort gate, we retraced our original route for six kilometres before heading west, following the "Spences Bridge" signs. At the time of writing, this route joined the new logging road at km 6.6 and followed it for about a 100 metres before leaving it to continue the downward run to the Nicola River and Highway 8 at Shackan (14 Mile).

The road is rough, sandy in some sections and coated with a layer of fist-size B.C. pea-gravel in others. By the time the road crosses Skuhun Creek at km 8.0, the lodgepole pine stands are beginning to thin out, replaced by interior Douglas fir and ponderosa pine. After swinging away from the creek for a few kilometres, it switchbacks down to the valley floor and passes the remnants of an old homestead at km 15.9. Where the road parallels the creek bed, the growth is lush and green. But the semi-desert climate is soon apparent where it crosses the benches. Scattered ponderosa pine, kinnikinnick and bunchgrass are all that survive the hot summer winds that blow up the valley.

Bev Veale's Kinnikinnick Homestead (km 20.5) is one of the few visible signs of human inhabitation along the route. Bev tried to use her ranch as a basis for cross-country skiing, but the warm winter winds of the past half dozen years kept taking away her snow. The Skuhun Creek road joins the Pimainus Ridge forest road at km 26.0. Another relatively new addition to the plateau back-roads, this one provides access to the Pimainus Lake area—and another possible backroads adventure.

The final three kilometres to Shackan on Highway 8, 24 km east of Spences Bridge, is good gravel road through Indian Reserve. If you decide to drive into Chataway Lake from the west, watch for the "Chataway" signs at Highway 8 and at the Pimainus Ridge junction—the rest of the trip is almost foolproof.

●●●

Fig. 31: Roscoe Lake from Roscoe Bluff.

Chataway Trails

Statistics   **For maps, see pages 134, 138, & 139.**

Topo Maps: Mamit Lake 92 I/7 (1:50,000).
Forest Maps: Merritt - Princeton.
Communities: Merritt & Logan Lake.

The upland plateau surrounding Chataway Lake is honey-combed with logging, mining exploration and lake access roads, as well as a variety of trails. Some of the trails date back to the late 1800s when Skuhun Creek was one of the routes from the Nicola Valley to the Cariboo. Other trails were used by prospectors hauling out the first copper ore mined in the Highland Valley.

While the old pack trails have all but disappeared in most places, portions of them have been rejuvenated and new trails have been cut into a few points of interest on the plateau. Much of the trail-making has been undertaken by Bill Roddy and his crew at Chataway Lakes Lodge, but indications are that the B.C. Forest Service will become more involved with recreation trail construction and maintenance in the area.

Antler Lake, northeast of Chataway Lake, (see map page 134) is accessible by a rough road and trail from Dot Lake or the Billy Lake Road. The simplest route is from Dot Lake, about three kilometres southeast of Chataway Lake. At one time, the Chataway resort had outpost camps at the north and south ends of Dot Lake, but now the south camp is a private residence and the north camp is a Forest Service recreation site.

The road to the north end of Dot Lake is rough, but the 2.5 km road into the Antler Lake trail head is even rougher. Practical for narrow 4x4's with good clearance only, it is probably better hiked than driven. From the trail head to the lake is a well marked 20-min-ute hike through the open timber. Motors are not permitted on Antler, but Chataway resort has several rowboats at the lake that can be rented in advance.

When we hiked in, a pair of float-tube fly fishermen were enjoy-ing the warm afternoon sun while drifting lazily on one of the lake's many finger-like bays.

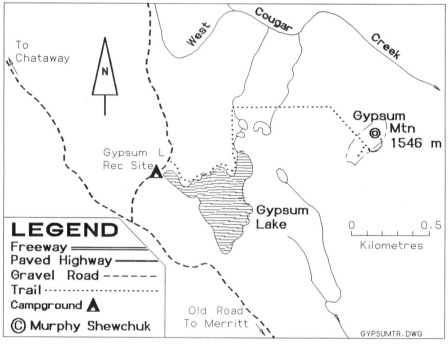

Map 19: Gypsum Mountain Trail.

Gypsum Mountain,(see map page 138) east of Gypsum Lake and almost due south of Antler Lake, is the site of another walking trail. Although I had not yet tackled this one at the time of writing, information I received from Bill Roddy of Chataway lodge and Lorne Robertson, Recreation Officer for the Merritt Forest District, indicates that it is an easy and enjoyable hike to an excel-lent viewpoint. Forest Service maps show it as a two hour, four kilometre round trip from the Gypsum Lake recreation site to the 1546 metre high peak.

Echo (Knight) Lake(see map page 139) lies to the northwest of Chataway Lake and a short walk to the west of Roscoe

Lake. Roscoe Lake, at 1585 metres, is one of the highest fishing lakes in the region. It is also shallow in places, with a boulder-strewn bottom. The Forest Service recreation site at the south end of Roscoe Lake is six kilometres northwest of Chataway lodge over a narrow gravel road with numerous rough, loose sections. Although there is always someone who will prove otherwise, may I suggest that a 4x4 is necessary to get to Roscoe.

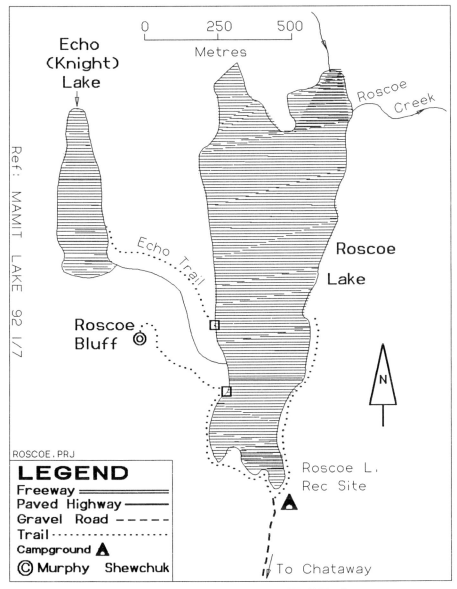

Map 20: Echo Lake / Roscoe Bluff Trails.

Bill Roddy of Chataway Lodge tells of several unusual but similar experiences that hikers have had at Echo (Knight) Lake. In one instance, a young couple were fly-fishing there when they suddenly decided to cut short their stay and return to the lodge. They did not compare their reasons for wanting to leave until later in the evening. When they did, they found that both had felt a strange, cold chill down their backs at exactly the same moment. In another example that Bill relates, an experienced young hiker was enjoying the beauty of the sheltered lake when she suddenly felt cold shivers and an aura of something supernatural. This woman, who had calmly faced bears and other wildlife, panicked and ran for ten minutes before regaining her composure.

Bill Roddy does not quite suggest that there are ghosts at Echo Lake, but he does concede that the strange silence surrounding it is hard for some city folk to accept.

The trail from Roscoe Lake to Echo (Knight) Lake is an easy 10-minute hike through the pines. It is marked with a large "E" where it leaves the western lake shore a few hundred metres north of the Roscoe Lake parking area. The easy way to reach the trail head is to paddle a canoe along the west shore of Roscoe Lake. The hiking and game trails along the lake shore, though occasionally hampered by windfalls, are not particularly difficult to follow if a canoe is not available.

Chataway lodge staff have recently cleared a trail into Roscoe Bluff, just south of Knight Lake. At the time of writing, this trail was well-marked with yellow-painted aluminium triangles. The trail leaves Roscoe Lake just south of the Knight Lake starting point and winds through the trees to the base of the bluff, before circling around to the north as it climbs to the crest.

If your timing is right, you may find ripe wild raspberries among the boulders at the base of the bluff and a view from the top that is well worth the 10 minute hike.

● ● ●

Promotory Mtn Road

Statistics	For map, see page 142.
Distance:	13.5 km, Highway 8 to Forest Lookout.
Travel Time:	One half hour.
Condition:	Gravel, rough in places.
Season:	June through October.
Topo Maps:	Merritt 92 I/2 (1:50,000).
Forest Maps:	Merritt - Princeton.
Communities:	Merritt & Lower Nicola.

Fig. 32: Wild Rose on Promontory Mountain.

The Forest Service fire lookout on 1734-m-high Promontory Mountain offers one of the best views in the Merritt area. The Cascades, the Coast Range, the Cariboo Mountains and the Monashees are all visible from the catwalk of the lookout.

The rough 13.5-km gravel road to the Promontory Mountain lookout leaves Highway 8, 11 km northeast of Merritt. It climbs through an old burn and then through stands of pine, fir and aspen. Side roads lead to hayfields and a homestead, but the major junctions are marked with simple "L/0" signs. The road is seldom open to the top before mid-May. In dry weather it is passable by car or light truck with ample clearance.

● ● ●

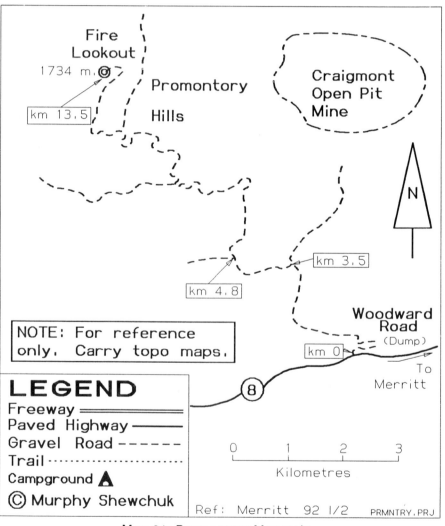

Map 21: Promontory Mountain.

Stoyoma Mountain Trails

Statistics   **For map, see page 145.**

Distance:	40 km, Highway 8 to Cabin Lake.
Travel Time:	Two to three hours.
Elevation gain:	ll5Om
Condition:	Gravel, rough sections on Stoyoma Mtn.
Season:	June through September.
Topo Maps:	Boston Bar 92H/14 (1:50,000).
	Prospect Creek 92I/3 (1:50,000).
Forest Maps:	Merritt - Princeton.
Communities:	Merritt & Lower Nicola.

Stoyoma Mountain is, at 2282 metres, one of the highest mountains on the north slope of the Cascade Mountains. At least a half dozen lakes are nestled in the folds of Stoyoma's slopes, and a maze of cattle and sheep trails wind through the alpine and subalpine timber. Stoyoma is also home to one of the few resident mountain goat populations in the region.

An access road was cut to Cabin Lake by local ranchers many years ago and is still passable on foot or horseback—or with a short-wheel-base four-wheel-drive vehicle with good clearance. Weyerhaeuser Canada Ltd.'s Merritt operation is currently logging on the southeast slopes of Stoyoma. Their roads provide easy access to the 1700 m level for the weekend traveller. Snow and spring washouts may keep the upper reaches of the road closed until the latter part of June and early snowstorms can make it dangerous again in October.

To find Stoyoma Mountain, drive 20 km west of Merritt on Highway 8, then follow the Petit Creek Road south and up Spius Creek ("Petit" Creek seems to no longer apply). Keep right at the junction near km 3—the road to the left returns to Highway 8 as the west end of Sunshine Valley Road.

For a diversion, you can turn off the main road at Davidson Road and follow it past Twisted Pine Ranch down to Spius Creek and Little Box Canyon. The road is good gravel, though somewhat narrow for the first 1.6 km. For the next three kilometres, it is narrow, twisting and very slippery when wet. Spius Creek makes a sharp bend through a rock cut at little box canyon, creating an excellent swimming hole. Cattle and game trails lead upstream to another good swimming hole. There is also a Forest Service recreation site across the river that is accessible from Jack Swartz Road.

Spius Creek has cut a fairly narrow canyon throughout its length and the road stays above the canyon, passing cattle and sheep ranches along the way. There are two side roads at a junction near the Prospect Creek bridge at km 24. Keep to the left at both junctions, and begin the steep climb out of the valley on the most used road. The road levels off somewhat near km 31, having climbed over 500 metres since the Prospect Creek bridge. It crosses another clear, cold creek near km 34.5—an excellent spot to fill your water bottles if you haven't already done so.

The kilometre signs nailed to trees along the route serve as a guide. Just beyond the 35K sign (tacked to a tree or stump well above the road), a side road climbs to the right. Take it and watch for a junction 0.8 km farther along. The road straight ahead continues into logging areas on the lower slopes of the mountain. Nestled in a hollow five minutes walk from a log landing two kilometres along this road is beautiful Lightning Lake. The trail into Lightning Lake is steep, but has been driven with a 4x4 vehicle.

If Cabin Lake or Stoyoma Mountain is your destination, take a right turn at the junction 0.8 km off the main road and follow the road through a logged strip and into a timber buffer zone, keeping left at a junction at 1.3 km. Just as the road emerges from the buffer strip, (km 2.3) an older road skirts the edge of the uppermost logged area and climbs through the trees to the west.

This is the original cattle and sheep trail into Cabin Lake. For most two-wheel-drive vehicles, this is a good place to park and start walking. With a 4x4, you may be able to continue the remaining 3.5 km to Cabin Lake, but turnaround space is limited.

Cabin Lake takes its name from an ancient log cabin that sits on a point that juts into the lake. Despite its elevation of 1860 metres, Cabin Lake can occasionally be warm enough for swimming in mid-summer. A Forest Service recreation site at the lake can be a good base for a Stoyoma Mountain ramble. Come equipped with good shoes, good maps and plenty of time.

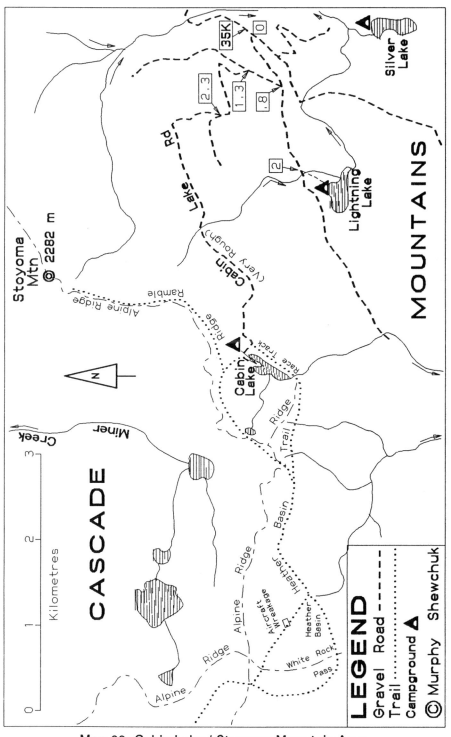

Map 22: Cabin Lake / Stoyoma Mountain Area.

Fig. 33: Cabin Lake and Stoyoma Mountain.

One trail worth exploring leads into a basin to the southwest of Cabin Lake where a water bomber crashed a number of years ago. The trail begins near the outlet of the lake and, after a short, steep climb, follows along the mountain slopes through the timber. It ends at the base of several scree slopes. If you look up to the north, you may be able to see the wreckage part way up the mountain side.

On your way back, you can climb up and over the crest of the ridge through one of the meadows nearer the lake and ramble back down along the creeks that feed into Cabin Lake. Watch carefully, and you may find one of the game trails that lead downhill around the rock outcroppings and through the timber. Look southwest from the top of the ridge on a clear day and you may be able to see the snow-capped peak of Mount Baker on the distant horizon.

Stoyoma Ridge is also easily reached from Cabin Lake or from almost any meadow along the last stretch of road into the lake. The subalpine timber is sparse and provides little opposition to the determined explorer. Although not particularly difficult, the round trip from 1860 metre Cabin Lake to the 2282 metre peak will take the better part of a day. Carry drinking water, as safe water may be in short supply along the ridge.

•••

History

Early Indian History

Interior Salish Indians have inhabited British Columbia for approximately 7,000 to 9,000 years, possibly having followed the retreating glaciers northward. They were initially year-round nomads, and it was not until about 3,000 years ago that they began spending the winters in pit-house communities.

Evidence of pit-houses remains in the form of circular depressions at selected campsites near major lakes and streams. The pit-house., or kekuli, was constructed by excavating a circular pit one metre deep and up to 10 m in diameter. Sturdy posts were set near the centre to support a framework of logs and poles which was then covered with soil. An opening at the top of the dome-shaped home served as a chimney and entrance. Pit-house depressions can be seen at Monck Provincial Park, on the north shore of Nicola Lake.

James A. Teit, a leading Indian authority and a resident of Merritt at the time of his death in 1922, suggested in his writing that the earliest permanent inhabitants of the Nicola Valley were a small tribe of Athabaskans. These Indians were closely related to the Chilcotins, and may have migrated southward from a base in the Mackenzie River region. They occupied almost all of the Nicola and Similkameen valleys but were soon challenged by the Thompson and Okanagan Salish Indians.

According to Teit, the Salish had originally migrated northward from what is now Washington, Idaho, Montana and Oregon. The Thompson Salish main settlement was at Lytton. As their numbers grew, they left this village at the confluence of the Thompson and Fraser rivers and moved up the Nicola River, establishing communities throughout most of the lower Nicola and upper Similkameen. The Okanagan Salish appear to have spread from the south Okanagan into the lower Similkameen and, via the north Okanagan, into the upper reaches of the Nicola River on the Douglas Plateau.

The Athabaskans fought the encroachment of the Okanagans but were eventually absorbed through intermarriage by the Thompson Salish, losing their language and identity.

At the time of the arrival of the first fur traders, the main Indian communities were at the present site of Merritt; at the foot of Nicola Lake; near Quilchena; and at Douglas Lake. Alexander Ross, then under the employ of the U.S. based Pacific Fur Company, is believed to have been the first white trader to visit the Nicola Valley. Ross and a companion were returning to Fort Okanogan in January 1813, following a Christmas visit to the recently established post at what is now Kamloops. They ran into difficulty with deep, crusted snow on the plateau country. After several days of very slow travel and an incident involving a powder horn that exploded while they were trying to start a fire, they were assisted by the Indians who wintered near Douglas and Nicola lakes.

For the next half century, fur traders from the Pacific Fur Company, the North West Company, and the Hudson's Bay Company successively maintained an amicable, though sometimes paternal, relationship with Indians of the district.

Among the most powerful of the Nicola Valley Indians that the fur traders dealt with was Walking Grizzly Bear (Hwistesmetxeqen) whom they referred to by the more manageable name of Nicholas. The natives had difficulty with Nicholas and shortened it to N'kuala or Nicola. Chief Nicola, an Okanagan Salish from Douglas Lake, gained the respect of both the Indians and the whites. His name appears repeatedly on maps of the period, suggesting that he had influence over most of the region from the Thompson River to the Okanagan Valley. Nicola's name still lives in the valley's largest lake and main river.

The Brigade Trails

The Hudson's Bay Company horse brigades must have been a magnificent sight as they filed through the Nicola Valley and over the mountain passes of the North Cascades. History tells us that from the first light of day until the heat of the afternoon sun, the trail was alive with the sounds of snorting horses and plodding hooves. The smell of hard-earned sweat permeated the air and the heavy diamond-hitched loads swayed in cadence with the songs of the voyageurs. A traveller of the day would certainly have stood in awe at the sight of 400 horses and 50 men winding along the trail.

Leading the procession was the guide, the trader or factor, and the clerks. At a respectful distance followed a white lead mare, adorned with a bell. Packers, frequently Indians, spread themselves out along the line of horses, each in charge of five to ten animals. At the rear was a rag-tag band that often included packers' families and other travellers.

For half a century, the brigade trails were the routes of trade and commerce in the interior of British Columbia. The waterways that served the fur traders in eastern Canada were not navigable in this land of high mountains and wild rivers. Horses and men were the sole movers of furs and trade goods in southwestern British Columbia from 1811 until the 1860s.

The colorful history of the fur brigades began in 1811 when Astorians David Stuart and Ovid de Montigny, of the New York based Pacific Fur Company, entered what is now British Columbia. They travelled north from Fort Okanogan, on the Columbia River, to the junction of the North and South Thompson rivers. Where the city of Kamloops stands today, they spent the winter among a large community of Shuswap Indians. In the following year, they were joined by Alexander Ross, and established Shuswap Fort, an American fur trading post well within Canada's present boundaries. In the same year, the Montreal-based North West Company established Thompson's River Post nearby. The two rival companies coexisted amicably until the Nor'Westers bought out the Astorians in 1813.

It was not until after the merger of the North West Company and the Hudson's Bay Company in 1821 that heavy use of the brigade routes was made. The route north of Kamloops followed the east side of the North Thompson River to Little Fort before striking westward across the upland lake country. From Horse Lake, near 100 Mile House, the trail wound northward following the approximate route of Highway 97 to Williams Lake, then north to the Fraser River at Fort Alexandria. This was the south end of the upper Fraser River navigation, and from Fort Alexandria the canoe became the mode of transportation to Fort George and Fort St. James. South of Kamloops, the horse brigades followed the South Thompson Riverup to Monte Creek and then proceeded south to Okanagan Lake along the approximate route of Highway 97. They then followed the western slopes of the Okanagan Valley until they reached the Columbia River.

In 1842, Fort Kamloops was erected on the west side of the North Thompson River and a new route established to the north country. It followed the north side of Kamloops Lake to Deadman Creek, then proceeded northward via Brigade Creek, Loon Lake and

Green Lake, joining the earlier trail at the west end of Horse Lake. This continued to be an important transportation artery until the Cariboo Wagon Road was completed in the mid-1860s.

The Oregon Treaty, signed in 1846, established the 49th Parallel as the boundary between Canada and the United States. While the treaty settled a long-standing international dispute, it created a whole new set of problems for the Hudson's Bay Company. Although the treaty allowed free navigation of the Columbia River, the Hudson's Bay Company, long a law unto themselves, found Fort Vancouver, their main establishment, under foreign control. Indian difficulties, border disputes and an irksome duty soon persuaded The Company that a new route to the Pacific was absolutely essential.

Alexander Caulfield Anderson was given the task of finding a satisfactory route from Fort Kamloops to the navigable waters of the lower Fraser River. After rejecting a western bypass of the Fraser Canyon via Seton, Anderson and Harrison lakes in 1846, Anderson sought a route that roughly paralleled the present Hope Princeton Highway (Hwy 3) for 40 km and then headed north across the mountains at Snass Creek.

But when Chief Factor James Douglas did not feel this route was feasible, Anderson began mapping a route from the head of lower Fraser River navigation at Yale, up the west side of the river to Spuzzum. Here he crossed the river, then began a steep climb up the mountainside a short distance north of Alexandra. His trail took him over the cliffs of the Fraser Canyon and down to the Anderson River which he followed upstream to Uztlius Creek before crossing the divide into the Nicola Watershed. After crossing Maka Creek, Anderson's trail dropped into the Coldwater Valley just south of Midday Creek. He followed the Coldwater River downstream to its junction with the Nicola River, where Merritt stands today. From this point he followed the general route of Highway 5A to Fort Kamloops.

More Indian difficulties south of the border forced the Hudson's Bay Company to abandon the Columbia River posts. Ovid Allard and his men established Fort Yale in the spring of 1848, in anticipation of the first brigades to use the new Anderson trail. The arrival of the outgoing brigade of 1848 was not a time of the usual joy and celebration. The trip from the Forks (Merritt) had taken 10 days, during 7 of which the horses were without food. The crossing of the Fraser near Spuzzum was a near disaster with many of the horses swept away by the boiling current. The incoming brigade of

1848 was even more difficult. The men fought a hard battle to get the canoes up the Fraser to Fort Yale. The river crossing at Spuzzum was even worse than on the previous trip partly because of the freshet and partly because hundreds of curious Indians interrupted their salmon fishing to "inspect" this strange group.

Douglas ordered the route abandoned, and work started on a trail explored by Henry Peers in 1848. In the spring of 1849, a fur trading post was established at the mouth of the Coquihalla River, now the town of Hope. While construction was underway, the outward brigade made the last trip over the Anderson trail.

Leaving the Fraser at Fort Hope, the inward Brigade of 1849 headed almost due east, avoiding the lower canyon of the Coquihalla and then following the river upstream until the junction with Peers Creek. The trail stayed on the north side of Peers Creek, following it up to the headwaters before making the steep climb to the top of Manson Ridge. The descent through Fools Pass and down to the Sowaqua was murderous and claimed many an errant horse. After crossing the Sowaqua, the trail climbed up and over 1,850-m-high Mount Davis. The steep, rocky ascent from Campement du Chevreuil to Palmer Pond on Mount Davis was probably the worst of the trip. From Palmer Pond, the trail descended into the headwaters of Podunk Creek, following it to the Tulameen River. The brigade avoided the worst of the Tulameen Canyon by following Blackeyes' Trail across Lodestone Mountain to Campement des Femmes, near the village of Tulameen.

The horse brigade had conquered the Cascade Mountains. Another day's travel north through the Otter Valley and they were into the Nicola Watershed near Aspen Grove. The route along the west side of Quilchena Creek was easy compared to the Cascades, and when they reached Nicola Lake they were well into the open grasslands. They climbed out of the valley floor near Napier Lake, angling to the west and passing through the open country near Brigade and McLeod lakes before descending into the Thompson Valley at Kamloops.

From the first outward brigade of 1848 until the completion of the Harrison-Lillooet Road and the Cariboo Wagon Road, the brigade trails through the Nicola Valley were an extremely important route of communications and commerce. Fur traders, gold seekers, politicians and farmers used these corridors through the mountains and plateau country. Such famous men as A.C. Anderson, Sir James Douglas and Sir Matthew Baillie Begbie passed this way on their journey into the history books of British Columbia.

Although numerous mentions of the trails have appeared in books, magazine articles and newspaper stories since the last brigades plodded over the mountains, it is only since the 1960s that serious effort has been made to relocate the old trails. Much of this effort has been expended in the North Cascade Mountains between Hope and Tulameen where the some of the axe blazes of more than a century ago remain.

The trail from the headwaters of Peers Creek to the top of Lodestone Mountain is now marked. The trip, a challenge to even the most experienced backpacker, takes as much as a week and is best travelled from mid-July to mid-September with an experienced guide.

The Okanagan Similkameen Parks Society (P.O. Box 787, Summerland, B.C. VOH IZO) is one of several organizations that has worked hard to have the old trails of the North Cascade Mountains preserved as part of our national heritage.

Settlement

Details are sketchy, but it is generally believed that Jesus Garcia, a Mexican packer on his way to the goldfields of the Cariboo, was the first to bring cattle and sheep into the Nicola Valley. Garcia brought his herd through the perilous Coquihalla Pass in 1860, and spent the winter at Spanish Springs, now Godey Creek, on the east boundary of the city of Merritt.

When the first permanent settlers drifted into the valley in the late 1860s, they quickly realized the agricultural potential. Hardy pioneers such as John Clapperton and Edwin Dalley helped establish a thriving community at the foot of Nicola Lake. Unlike many of the gold rush towns that these men had passed through, Nicola became a community of substance. Stores, livery stables, a school and a church were constructed. As the community grew, a sawmill and flour mill became the basis for local industry.

In 1882, Michael Hagan, then editor of the Yale-based Inland Sentinel, reported visiting Nicola on a return trip from Kamloops. "...we were at Fenson's Mills, and here it was we beheld the most business-looking place after leaving Kamloops. The mill power for both the grist mill and saw mill, where also a planer and shingle arrangement were to be seen, was from a fine stream running from the Nicola River."

Elsewhere in the valley, small settlements were springing up at Lower Nicola, Quilchena, Moore's (at the north end of Nicola Lake) and Forksdale (now Merritt).

Fig. 34: Murray Church at Nicola, B.C.

Transportation was a problem in the early days, and in 1874, more than 90 residents of the southern Interior were petitioning the British Columbia Lieutenant Governor: "The undersigned settlers of the Kamloops, Okanagan, Nicola and Cache Creek Valleys, beg to petition Your Honor, for the construction of a road from the South end of Nicola Forks, up the Coldwater Valley to the summit of the Coquhalla [sic], thence down the Coquhalla to Fort Hope. The distressed condition of the stockraisers of the district, owing to their having no outlet by which they can drive to the now almost only beef market in the Province, together with the fact that the cattle ranges are becoming overstocked and destroyed, we trust will induce you to make some efforts for our relief."

The decade of the seventies was a period of road building in the Nicola Valley. The wagon road from Spences Bridge was completed in 1875. In 1876, the ranchers' pleas were heeded and the Hope Trail was built through the Coldwater Valley and Coquihalla Canyon, improving local access to the growing beef markets of the lower mainland. The wagon road from Kamloops to Nicola was built in 1877-78, opening the ranch country to the north to carriage traffic.

The construction of the Canadian Pacific Railway in the 1880s provided a vast new market for Nicola Valley beef. This sparked the growth of the Douglas Lake Cattle Company with, as its nucleus, land originally homesteaded by John Douglas in 1872. Today the Douglas Lake Ranch claims to be the largest in Canada, running 15,000 Hereford cattle on 222,000 hectares of grasslands, lakes and timber.

Dan McGinnis, a young man of 19 when he trekked into the valley in June, 1883, wrote of the hardships faced by early ranchers in getting their cattle to the railway crews and lower mainland markets.

"I made two trips a month, taking 150 head each trip," wrote McGinnis. "Accompanied by five Indians, I would drive the cattle through the Coquihalla Pass to Hope. This trail was barely wide enough for the cattle to walk in single file. On one side rose a wall of rock, and on the other side was a sheer drop of 300 feet. On this trail was a narrow bridge of three logs, off which many of the cattle fell, and I lost as many as eleven steers in one trip."

The first mention of Nicola Valley coal appeared in the New Westminster British Columbian in 1869, where it was stated that blacksmiths on the Cariboo Wagon Road were using valley coal brought out by packhorse. Test holes were drilled near the confluence of the Nicola and Coldwater rivers in 1892-93. The results were "far beyond expectations" and lobbying for a railway into the valley increased in tempo.

In the early 1900s, William Hamilton Merritt held a government charter for the Nicola, Kamloops and Similkameen Coal and Railway Company. W.H. Merritt had the authority to construct a rail line from Chilliwack to Spences Bridge via the Coquihalla, Coldwater and Nicola valleys. A townsite named Forksdale was surveyed before W.H. Merritt's plans fell through.

Fig. 35: Fallslake Creek Bridge in Coquihalla Canyon.

In 1904, John Hendry staked 1,100 hectares of coal rights southwest of Forksdale with the intentions of starting a colliery. Hendry had already made his fortune in Vancouver as owner of Hastings Mills, and it was said he had good connections with the Canadian Pacific Railway. When the CPR extension was completed into the valley in 1907, the coal mining community of Forksdale was renamed in honor of W.H. Merritt.

A report in a July 1909 issue of Saturday Sunset summed up the situation. "Merritt, B.C., a new town in the Nicola Valley has a population of 500-800 souls. It has seven stores, three hotels, a railway, a couple of coal mines, livery stables, billiard parlor, cafes, opera house, bank and newspaper, but it has neither a church nor a railway station."

A church was still in the future, but work was started on the railway station the following month.

This was the era of coal and the steam locomotive, and railroad construction continued across southern British Columbia. The search for a route for a Coast-to-Kootenay railway led to renewed interest in the Coquihalla region. After numerous surveys and false starts, the Kettle Valley Railway started carving a railway right-of-way down the Coquihalla Canyon. Andrew McCulloch is justly credited with the greatest feat of railway engineering up to that time, building 32 bridges in 65 km.

"Six of the bridges are steel, three of them are bridges that are as big as any in this country," said a 1915 report in the Merritt Herald. "The remaining 26 bridges are to be built of wood and over six million feet of timber will be used."

In 1916, after almost two decades of construction delays, the last spike was driven on the famous Kettle Valley Railway. For more than four decades, the Coast-to-Kootenay rail line faced the snow and ice of the Coquihalla Canyon. The Coquihalla link was finally broken by a giant mud slide in 1959, the last shot in the battle against Nature and declining revenues. A portion of the renowned KVR remained a CPR spur line linking Penticton with the main line at Spences Bridge until May, 1989 when the last lumber train rolled down the tracks. (At the time of writing, a Rails to Trails group was lobbying to have the railway right-of-way converted to a recreational corridor.)

The first half of the twentieth century saw many changes in the Nicola Valley. The coal mines drew the centre of commerce away from Nicola, and Merritt grew at its expense. Then coal gradually lost favour as an energy source and highways replaced railways as the main transportation routes. These changes provided the occasional severe setback, but the valley did not die. Instead, lumbering, copper mining, ranching and tourism have all contributed to a steady, orderly growth.

Today Merritt is still the commercial centre of the Nicola Valley. Some of the 19th century settlements have disappeared while others, such as Nicola, have changed little. Landmarks including the Murray Church at Nicola, the Coldwater Hotel at Merritt, and the Quilchena Hotel serve as reminders of a colorful past: a past that is relived each Labour Day weekend in the rip-roaring celebration of the Nicola Valley Rodeo.

●●●

Physical Features

Fig. 36: Zopkios Ridge at the Coquihalla Summit.

The Coquihalla River begins northeast of Hope at the summit of the Coquihalla Pass. Its source, the Coquihalla Lakes, is surrounded by craggy mountain peaks, some reaching 2130 metres in elevation. As the river flows southward, it is joined by numerous small creeks and a few more significant waterways. Boston Bar Creek, the first major tributary, has its source in a mountain valley a short distance from the headwaters of the Coquihalla. It, however, flows to the west of Needle Peak, joining the Coquihalla downstream from the summit.

The Nicola River rises in the upland country of the Douglas Plateau, part of the much larger Thompson Plateau that separates the Coast Mountains to the west from the Monashee Mountains to the east. In its 150-km journey from its origins near Pennask Lake to the Thompson River at Spences Bridge, the Nicola has etched a path through a variety of climatic and topographic zones.

The pine-forested lake country where the river originates lies as much as 2,000 m above sea level. As it winds southwestward, the Nicola River passes through an ever-changing panorama of rolling natural bunchgrass. This is Douglas Lake Ranch country, famous for its Hereford cattle. The river soon widens to form Douglas Lake and then Nicola Lake. Two other important creeks drain the plateau country, emptying into Nicola Lake: Stumplake Creek empties the string of lakes to the north, and Quilchena Creek carries the water off the lake-studded plateau country to the southeast.

The Nicola River, lined with cottonwoods, cuts a meandering path through the hay fields on the way from Nicola Lake to the junction with the Coldwater River in the heart of Merritt. The Nicola's major tributary, the Coldwater rises in the North Cascade Mountains, west of the Coquihalla Lakes. Spire-like snow-capped mountain peaks, glacial silt-laden streams and steep timbered slopes present a sharp contrast to the plateau country. The natural grasslands that are so much a part of the Nicola Basin are not apparent in the Coldwater Valley. Instead, somewhat heavier rainfall and differing soil conditions have fostered heavier timber growth in the upper reaches of the U-shaped valley; nearer Merritt, scattered ponderosa pine is found.

From Merritt, the Nicola River strikes out in a northwesterly direction, following an ever-narrowing valley through the north slope of the Cascades. At first the valley floor is carpeted with small ranch holdings, irrigation sprinklers creating man-made rainbows over the alfalfa fields. But as the river nears the Thompson, the fields give way to steep, colorful canyon walls. Striking hoodoos stand guard over the tiny market gardens while outside the reach of cultivation, sagebrush and prickly pear cactus thrive.

I f you drive slowly up the Douglas Lake Road from the junction with Highway 5 at Nicola Lake just as the morning sun lights the hills you will see a segment of the physical history of the valley that dates back more than 100 centuries. Across the valley to the north, the morning shadows accentuate the shorelines of two ancient lakes that once filled the valley from ridge to ridge. The lower shoreline is visible behind the red-painted buildings of the Quilchena Cattle Company "Home Ranch" while the upper shoreline can be seen as you approach B.C. Hydro's Nicola substation.

During the last period of glaciation, which ended some 10,000 years ago, almost all British Columbia was covered by massive sheets of ice, often reaching thickness in excess of 1,500 m. Only the highest peaks escaped the grinding action of this flowing mass of destruction. The Thompson Plateau region was ripped open and reformed, leaving scars that the dry climate and open grasslands have preserved.

The many north-south lying chains of lakes indicate the direction of the ice movement. Drumlins and eskers, side and front moraines, and erratics such as the huge boulders in the open fields near the north end of Stump Lake, mark where the ice melted, depositing its heavy load.

The first major lake to form in the Nicola Basin as the glaciers began to melt was Glacial Lake Quilchena. It reached an elevation of approximately 1000 m above sea level and drained southward into the headwaters of Otter Creek near Aspen Grove. Shore features of this ancient lake are only visible in a few locations.

Glacial Lake Hamilton was formed when the ice plug retreated in the Salmon River Valley permitting eastward drainage through the Douglas Plateau. This lake was only about 70 m lower than Glacial Lake Quilchena, but some of its features are still visible in the form of the previously mentioned shoreline, and terraces on the north slope of Mount Hamilton, southeast of Nicola Lake.

The last of the giant glacial lakes was Lake Merritt. It was formed when the ice melted out of the Campbell Creek Valley to the north and allowed the meltwater to drain into the Thompson Valley east of Kamloops. The lake level was restricted by a hard layer of bedrock located between Stump and Napier lakes, alongside Highway 5A. A significant canyon was carved into the reddish rock as Glacial Lake Merritt spilled over this outcropping. As the warming climate forced the giant ice sheet northward, the last ice plug melted out of the northwestern (lower) reaches of the Nicola River, opening the present drainage route out of the valley.

Beneath the grasslands, lakes and forests of the Thompson Plateau and the North Cascade Mountains lies a stone heart of great richness and variety. The plateau country contains sedimentary and volcanic formations into which have intruded stocks of granitic rock. Flat or gently sloping ancient lava beds obscure even older rock formations. These lava beds often underlie the step-like slopes and the large unbroken plateau areas. Coal deposits and fossil beds in the immediate Merritt area are evidence of the age of some of the rock formations. As will be discussed in the section on settlement, these coal deposits once played a significant part in the development of the valley.

The Serpentine Belt which crosses the North Cascades from the vicinity of Ladner Creek in Coquihalla Canyon to just north of Boston Bar on the Fraser, is a mineral-rich zone. Carolin Mines, which has workings near Ladner Creek, was considered to have the potential of a large tonnage gold mine. Other known minerals in this region include silver, lead, iron, zinc, copper and molybdenum. Rockhounds and artists find the Serpentine Belt of interest because of the nephrite jade and soapstone deposits that are found in conjunction with serpentine.

The most significant geological feature of the Nicola Valley is the Guichon Creek Batholith. This 200-million-year-old intrusion of plutonic rock extends from Merritt to Cache Creek and contains some of British Columbia's largest deposits of low grade copper and molybdenum. The former Craigmont Mine near Merritt and the world-class open pit mines of the Highland Valley are situated on the batholith. (See the Highland Valley Road section for details.)

●●●

Climate and Vegetation

Cactus and columbine, sagebrush and cedar. These may be unlikely plant combinations, but they are all found in Coquihalla Country, often within hiking distance of each other. The Nicola drainage basin, with its widely varied terrain and elevation range, lends itself to an extended mixture of climate zones and, consequently, a diverse flora.

In general, the Thompson Plateau has a continental climate. The winters are moderately cold and the summers hot. Winter temperatures at Merritt, for instance, range from -30 degrees Celsius to 0 degrees Celsius and temperatures during July and August easily reach 30 degrees Celsius and occasionally may go as high as 40 degrees Celsius. Annual precipitation varies from 15 cm to 75 cm; the average at Merritt is 30 cm. Temperature and precipitation variations are closely related to elevation.

Snowfall is usually light in the main valleys with most of the precipitation falling in the form of rain in the spring months. The vegetation at the lower altitudes is typical of a hot, dry climate with sagebrush, bunchgrass, rabbit bush and ponderosa pine being the natural dominant species. A close look at the ground in the early spring may reveal sage buttercups, yellow bells, shooting stars and a variety of other tiny wildflowers. In late April and early May, the sunflower-like blossoms of arrowleaf balsamroot turn the otherwise drab hillsides into a field of yellow. They are soon joined by the white blossoms of saskatoon bushes, fields of blue lupines and then a color kaleidoscope that includes yellow arnica, red and pink wild roses, rose-purple sticky geranium, lavender blue penstemon and other flowers including the pale yellow prickly pear cactus.

As the elevation and rainfall increases, the ponderosa pine give way to stands of interior Douglas-fir. Trembling aspen and cottonwood thrive along the creek beds and in the wetter hollows. The flowering plants change, too, though the transition may not be as distinct. Wild strawberry, Oregon grape, stonecrop, fireweed, western columbine and Columbian lily are but a few that add their beauty to the landscape in spring and summer.

Snowfall is usually heavier at the higher elevations of the plateau country. As much as one metre of snow can accumulate over the winter, but warm chinook winds often strip bare the lowland valleys and exposed slopes.

The Coquihalla Valley, which is part of the freeway route linking Hope and Merritt through the North Cascades, is an area of heavy snowfall. Records kept when the Kettle Valley Railway was operating (1916-1963) indicate that snow accumulations of over 12 m were not uncommon and, in years of heavy fall, snow depths reached 15 m. The most pronounced climatic transition in the region takes place in the southern portion of the Coquihalla Valley where average annual precipitation changes from 100 cm to 40 cm in less that 24 km.

The subalpine zone that makes up much of the North Cascades and portions of the Thompson Plateau is covered by subalpine fir and Engelmann spruce. Shrubs and berry bushes are plentiful, including tasty huckleberries and wild strawberries. Many of the wildflowers that grow on the lower slopes can be found in even greater profusion in logged areas, old burns and snowslide paths. Indian paintbrush in a variety of colors, yellow and purple violets, wine-red monkey flower and yellow avalanche lilies all add their beauty to the spring and summer scene.

The alpine tundra that makes up a very small portion of the region is not as barren as it first appears. Many varieties of trees and flowering plants have adapted to the harsh winters and short summers. Some are adaptations of plants found at lower elevations while others are unique to the alpine environment. One of the more distinctive flowering plants found here is the western anemone. It forces its shoots up through the edges of the melting snow, quickly opens its leaves and then its blossoms to catch the warm rays of the sun. As the flower stem grows, its "towhead baby" seed pod is thrust into the wind where the parachute-like seeds are widely dispersed.

Ranching is the predominant form of agriculture in the Nicola Valley. Hay crops grow on the bottom land while cattle graze on the upland grass, sometimes into the alpine. During the winter, the cattle are driven down to the lowlands and fed hay produced during the previous summer. Irrigation is used to overcome the low moisture holding capacity of the sandy soils and to augment the limited summer rainfall. Thus man has modified the effects of climate and terrain in his attempt to wrest a living from the land.

Wildlife

Birds

The relatively mild climate and abundance of small lakes makes Coquihalla Country a paradise for birds. Estimates vary, but knowledgeable naturalists suggest that between 125 and 200 species of birds are at least seasonally present in the Thompson Plateau region.

Mid-winter bird counts carried out by members of the Kamloops Naturalist Club over the past decade have identified at least 90 species. The total number of birds counted in the specified four-hour count period have exceeded 3,000. Among the most common on these winter counts are Bohemian waxwings, starlings, house sparrows, snow buntings, mallard ducks, Canada geese and whistling swans. By far the predominant species are the whistling swans which winter on Shuswap Lake, the South Thompson River and, in mild winters, on Nicola Lake. These beautiful white birds have a wing length of up to 560 mm and weigh as much as 10 kg, placing them among the largest flying birds. They are likely to be mistaken only for their larger cousin, the trumpeter swan.

On one January count the Kamloops Naturalist Club reported 565 swans with at least 156 immatures. Twenty-four whistling swans, including eight immatures, were counted at the mouth of Quilchena Creek—the only open water on Nicola Lake at the time.

It would be impossible to do the Nicola Valley bird population justice in the limited space available in this book. However, the following season to season review will highlight some of those that I have observed.

Winter sightings include the whistling swans, great gray owls, the occasional snowy owl, various birds that frequent back-yard feeders and a stray blue heron that wanders the shores of the Nicola River. Spring brings a large number of bald and golden eagles, plus the occasional osprey. Canada geese and waterfowl are plentiful, particularly on the smaller lakes and ponds of the plateau country. The bright flash of the mountain bluebird is also a frequent sight, and nesting boxes have been set up on the grasslands east of Stump Lake to encourage these insect-eaters to stay. Chukkar partridge and several species of grouse are common throughout the region. They can most often be seen in the scattered timber in the summer and early autumn. In the autumn, the region becomes part of the migratory waterfowl flyway and ducks, geese and bobbing rafts of coots are a familiar sight on Nicola and Stump lakes.

Mammals

Few of the larger mammals of the Thompson Plateau and North Cascade Mountains live without some form of contact with man. Hunting is allowed in season and poaching is sometimes a problem. Because there are no large federal or provincial parks to offer sanctuary, the mammals tend to remain wary of man and his presence.

Despite this justified wariness, the most visible of the large mammals is the shy mule deer. This adaptable animal can be found throughout the region, from valley floor to alpine meadow. Mule deer are often seen in the early morning hours, drinking from a stream or feeding on the tender shoots of young aspen or cottonwood. Whitetail deer inhabit only a limited portion of the valley. In the summer months, their main habitat is the slopes of Promontory Mountain and the lower Guichon Creek valley northwest of Merritt. A small herd of whitetail deer is also know to frequent the Douglas Plateau to the north of Chapperon Lake.

Moose, although not originally native to the southern plateau country, migrated southward from central British Columbia as man opened up the heavy forest barrier of the north Cariboo with his logging, farming and roads. Moose are now dispersed throughout the plateau and are as likely to be seen in the open grasslands as in the upland swamps.

Mountain goats range the skyline ridges of the North Cascade Mountains. Stoyoma Mountain and the peaks of the upper Coldwater Valley, to the west of the Coquihalla Lakes, are the best places to catch a glimpse of these white ungulates.

Black and brown bear are relatively common in the Nicola basin, although they are generally wary of man and will usually run at the first sign of a confrontation. ("Usually" is the key word. Almost every animal will fight if it fears that it or its young are threatened.) Though seldom seen, there are still a few grizzly bears in the North Cascade Mountains.

Coyotes are the grassland scavengers. They feed on small animals and birds and sick calves or dead cattle. They are the most elusive of the grassland mammals: their bounding "bush" is often all that is seen as they dodge among the sagebrush. It is the lucky photographer who manages to "shoot" a coyote in the wild.

It is an even luckier photographer who manages to capture a mountain beaver on film. Not a true beaver, but a large primitive rodent up to 40 cm in length and weighing more than one kilogram, this nocturnal mammal lives near the slow moving watercourses of the Cascade rain forests. The mountain beaver habitat can be recognized by the neat stacks of bracken and other lush vegetation found drying outside their tunnel entrances. Though thought to be restricted to a small strip along the west coast of North America, sightings have been reported in both the Nicola and Coquihalla watersheds.

In all, some 50 species of mammals have been recorded in the region. In addition to those already named, others occasionally seen include cougar, lynx, beaver, weasel, mink, fox and, in the alpine, marmot, pika and bog lemmings.

Insects

The avid outdoor enthusiast has found Coquihalla Country refreshingly free of bothersome insects. Mosquitoes can be somewhat of a nuisance early in the season as can yellow-jacket wasps in late summer. Shy black widow spiders inhabit the darkness of some abandoned barns and cabins, but their bite is not considered dangerous at this northern latitude.

The hot dry summers and generally open terrain do not encourage mosquitoes, blackflies or horseflies. Most summer hiking and fishing trips can be accomplished with minimal use of insect repellent or special clothing, although both are good insurance.

One of the most feared and least understood creatures of the Nicola Valley is the Rocky Mountain or paralysis tick. Also known as the wood tick, it ranges in Canada from the British Columbia interior dry belt to Saskatchewan. In the Nicola Valley, the wood tick is misnamed, for it inhabits the open grasslands, preferring rocky southern exposures where the sun warms the earth early in the spring. From March to June, with peak activity in mid-April, ticks rest on the scrub vegetation and bunchgrass, awaiting the unwary warm-blooded passerby. Tick paralysis is a disease associated with the local tick, but symptoms usually occur only after the adult female Rocky Mountain tick has been feeding for about five days. There is no pain or fever as the paralysis starts with the body extremities and progresses towards the core. Complete recovery begins as soon as the tick is removed. If the tick is not removed, death can occur when the vital organs become paralyzed.

Recognition, protection and after-hike hygiene are the basic steps to avoiding tick problems. The adult female Rocky Mountain tick is reddish-brown with a white shield near her head. She is not much larger than a capital "O" on this page. Smooth pants tucked into boots help keep the tick from gaining a firm hold when it is brushed against. A close personal inspection, particularly under wristbands, clothing straps and body hair is necessary to remove any ticks that may have become attached.

If a tick appears to be firmly attached, it can usually be removed with a slow gentle pull. Unlike other varieties with barbed mouthpieces, the Rocky Mountain tick fastens itself to the skin with a whitish glue which usually comes off with the tick.

Amphibians and Reptiles

Coquihalla Country is home to an estimated 14 species of amphibians and reptiles, the most common of which are frogs and garter snakes. There have, however, been sightings of rattlesnakes and bull snakes near Spences Bridge and in the southeast near the Okanagan Valley, though seldom near populated areas. None of the trips outlined in this book is likely to place the hiker in contact with any dangerous snakes.

The bull snake is a shy reptile that would rather retreat than fight. However, when cornered, it will coil, emit a loud warning hiss, and bang its tail against the gravel to imitate a rattlesnake. If forced to strike, it is not poisonous but can inflict a painful bite.

The Northern Pacific rattlesnake has many of the same characteristics. Most reported bites have occurred when people inadvertently stepped on or handled a rattlesnake or when the snake was teased. As two-thirds of the bites occur on the feet and lower legs, boots and sturdy pants should be worn. Extra precautions should be taken when climbing to avoid accidentally putting your hand on a sunning snake.

In the event of rattlesnake bite, the important thing is to remain calm and quickly seek medical aid.

Fish and Fishing

The Thompson-Okanagan Fish and Wildlife management area attracts close to 50 per cent of British Columbia's total freshwater sports fishing activity. When we consider that this area comprises less than 10 per cent of the province, the figure becomes even more significant. As a freshwater sports fishery, the Thompson Plateau is unsurpassed in British Columbia. The Nicola Valley motto of "a lake a day as long as you stay" is no idle boast.

Fish, fresh or dried, were a year-round mainstay of the Indians that inhabited British Columbia prior to the arrival of the first fur traders. Then dried fish and fish oil became important items of barter and were often the winter staple at the Interior fur trading posts. Sockeye salmon were the most valuable fish in the river systems that included the Nass, Skeena and Fraser.

The salmon, and to a lesser extent the smaller species of fish, were thoroughly utilized by the native people. They were eaten fresh, or split and dried for use in winter. The roe was considered a delicacy and stored in special woven baskets for winter use. Fish heads were used as soup stock or in a mixture for tanning hides.

The Coquihalla River and the Coldwater-Nicola system were, and continue to be, important salmon spawning tributaries of the Fraser River. The smaller tributary streams also play host to the eggs of rainbow trout, Dolly Varden char and kokanee. The Coldwater River is a spawning channel for chinook and coho salmon, particularly the stretch of river upstream from Kingsvale.

Chapperon, Douglas and Nicola lakes were considered especially valuable by the Okanagan Indians because of their ample fish stocks and because the ice left them earlier than many other of the plateau lakes. Nicola Lake, noted for its depth, is said to harbour 26 varieties of fish, some weighing up to 9 kg: among them are mountain whitefish, spring salmon, kokanee, rainbow trout, Dolly Varden char, Pacific lamprey and freshwater ling cod.

Rainbow (or Kamloops) trout tend to overshadow all other game species sought by anglers. They make up more than 60 per cent of the catch on a province-wide basis. Rainbow trout are an even larger part of the freshwater angler's take in the Nicola Valley.

Serious fishermen have found that the best angling is in the lakes to the north of Highway 8 and east of Highway 5. These lakes are managed largely by stocking and habitat improvement. In a few selected lakes, fishing restrictions are being used as a management tool. The British Columbia Sport Fishing regulations should be consulted before angling in Coquihalla Country.

Fig. 37: Canoeing on Lac Le Jeune.

Bibliography

Books

AKRIGG, G.P.V. & Helen B. *1001 British Columbia Place Names* (Discovery Press, Vancouver, B.C. 1973)

AKRIGG, G.P.V. & Helen B. *British Columbia Chronicle, 1847-1871* (Discovery Press, Vancouver, B.C. 1977)

BULMAN, T. Alex. *Kamloops Cattlemen*, (Gray's Publishing, Sidney, B.C. 1972.)

FRYE, Alan. *The Burden of Adrian Knowle* (Doubleday, Toronto, Ont. 1974)

HARRIS, Bob, Harley Hatfield and Peter Tassie *The Okanagan Brigade Trail* (Vernon, B.C. 1989 ISBN 0-9694207-0-6)

MILLIKEN, A.C. "Paul Fraser's Grave". *BC Digest* (April, 1962) pp 59-60.

NICOLA VALLEY ARCHIVES ASSOCIATION *Merritt & the Nicola Valley: An Illustrated History.* (Sonotek Publishing Ltd., Box 1752, Merritt, B.C. 1989 ISBN 0-929069-01-3)

READ, Stanley E. *A Place Called Pennask*, (Mitchell Press, Vancouver, B.C. 1977)

ROTHENBURGER, Mel. *'We've Killed Johnny Ussher!'* (Mitchell Press, Vancouver, B.C. 1973.)

SANFORD, Barrie McCulloch's Wonder - The Story of the Kettle Valley Railway. Whitecap Books, West Vancouver, B.C. 1977

SHEWCHUK, Murphy O. *Backroads Explorer: Similkameen and South Okanagan.* (Hancock House, Surrey, B.C. 1988 ISBN 0-88839-205-2)

SHEWCHUK, Murphy O. *Backroads Explorer: Thompson-Cariboo* (Maclean Hunter, Vancouver, B.C. 1985 ISBN 0-88896-151-0)

SHEWCHUK, Murphy O. *The Craigmont Story* (Hancock House, Surrey, B.C. 1983 ISBN 0-88839-980-4)

SHEWCHUK, Murphy O. *Exploring the Nicola Valley* (Douglas & McIntyre, Vancouver, B.C. 1981 ISBN 0-88894-307-5)

SHEWCHUK, Murphy O. *Fur, Gold and Opals* (Hancock House, Surrey, B.C. 1975)

SMITH, Jessie Ann *Widow Smith of Spence's Bridge* (Sonotek Publishing Ltd., Box 1752, Merritt, B.C. 1989 ISBN 0-929069-00-5)

WOOLLIAMS, Nina G. *Cattle Ranch - The Story of the Douglas Lake Cattle Company* (Douglas & McIntrye, Vancouver B.C. 1979 ISBN 0-88894-217-6)

●●●

Additional information

Merritt-Princeton Forest Service Recreation Sites Map, available from Ministry of Forests, Bag 4400, Merritt, B.C. V0K 2B0 or, preferably, in person from their office at 2196 Quilchena Avenue, Merritt, B.C. Telephone (604) 378-9311.

Topographical maps can be obtained from Christian Book & Gift, 1951 Quilchena Avenue, P.O. Box 1486, Merritt, B.C. V0K 2B0. Telephone (604) 378-6633.

Provincial Parks of the Cariboo-Shuswap-Okanagan map/brochure. Ministry of Lands, Parks and Housing, Parks and Outdoor Recreation Division, 1019 Wharf Street, Victoria, B.C. V8W 2Y9

Park information is also available from BC Parks, Fraser Valley District, Box 10, Cultus Lake, B.C. V0X 1H0 or from BC Parks, Room 101, 1050 West Columbia St., Kamloops, B.C. V2C 1L4.

Hope Travel Infocentre, 919 Water Avenue, Hope, B.C. V0X 1L0. Telephone (604) 869-2021.

Kamloops Travel Infocentre, 10- 10th Avenue, Kamloops, B.C. V2C 6J7. Telephone (604) 374-3377.

Kelowna Travel Infocentre, 544 Harvey Avenue, Kelowna, B.C. V1Y 6C9. Telephone (604) 861-1515.

District of Logan Lake Travel Infocentre, Box 190, Logan Lake, B.C. V0K 1W0. Telephone (604) 523-6225.

Merritt & District Chamber of Commerce, P.O. Box 1649, Merritt, B.C. V0K 2B0. Telephone (604) 378-5634.

Index

About the Author

MURPHY SHEWCHUK has been writing and illustrating newspaper and magazine articles and books since the mid-1960s.

Born in Hamilton, Ontario, in 1943, he grew up in the B.C. mining town of Pioneer Gold Mines and developed a triple interest in outdoor exploring, photography and electronics while still a teenager. After a stint in the R.C.A.F. in eastern Canada, he moved back to B.C. to a job in electronics with writing and photography as his major interests. In 1971, his work took him to Kamloops B.C., where he began a weekly *Outdoor Scene* column for the *Kamloops Sentinel*. From the column, he moved to features in *BC Outdoors* and other magazines. He now lives in Merritt, B.C. with his wife Katharine and grand-daughter Bridget.

Fig. 38: Murphy Shewchuk.

More than 300 of his magazine articles and 1000 of his photographs have appeared in such publications as *Adventure Travel, BC Outdoors, Camping Canada, Canadian Geographic, Field & Stream, MotorHome, Photo Life, Skyword, Western Living,* and *Westworld.*

He has also published seven other books including; *Exploring Kamloops Country, Fur, Gold & Opals, Exploring the Nicola Valley, The Craigmont Story, Backroads Explorer Vol 1: Thompson-Cariboo* and *Backroads Explorer Vol 2: Similkameen & South Okanagan.*

In addition to his life-long interest in photography and exploring the mountains of western Canada, Murphy is a workshop speaker at writer's conferences across Canada and in the U.S.A. His writing and photography have received awards from the Outdoor Writers of Canada and the Macmillan Bloedel newspaper journalism competitions. Shewchuk was honoured with the Allen Sangster Award for contributions to the Canadian Authors Association in 1989.

●●●